Praying with Mary

Praying with Mary

Contemplating Scripture at Her Side

By
Robert Faricy, SJ
and
Lucy Rooney, SND de N

BOOKS & MEDIA
Boston

Library of Congress Cataloging-in-Publication Data

Faricy, Robert L., 1926–

Praying with Mary : contemplating Scripture at her side / Robert Faricy and Lucy Rooney.

p. cm.

ISBN 0-8198-5937-0 (pbk.)

1. Mary, Blessed Virgin, Saint—Prayer-books and devotions—English. I. Rooney, Lucy. II. Title.

BX2160.23 .F37 2002

242'.74—dc21

2002003637

Scripture used is the authors' translation.

English translation of the *Catechism of the Catholic Church* for the United States of America copyright © 1994, United States Catholic Conference, Inc.—Libreria Editrice Vaticana. Used with permission.

Cover Photo: *Annunciation.* Lorenzetti, Ambrogio (1319–1374) © Scala/Art Resource, NY

Original title: *Praying with Mary,* Copyright © 2000, St. Pauls, United Kingdom.

Printed and published in the U.S.A. by Pauline Books & Media, 50 Saint Pauls Avenue, Boston MA 02130-3491.

www.pauline.org

Pauline Books & Media is the publishing house of the Daughters of St. Paul, an international congregation of women religious serving the Church with the communications media.

1 2 3 4 5 6 7   07 06 05 04 03 02

Acknowledgements

We are grateful to the Sisters of Notre Dame
  of Namur,
as well as to the Jesuits of Marquette University
  in Milwaukee.
Above all, we thank our Lord Jesus Christ for
  grace in our lives, and his mother for praying
  for us and with us as we wrote this book.
Respectfully, we dedicate this book to the
  Immaculate Heart of Mary, the mother
  of Jesus.

Contents

Introduction

Mary and Jesus

Mary of Nazareth is the mother of Jesus. This makes her important to God, to all of us together, and to each one of us.

Christian tradition has always held that because Mary is the mother of Jesus she is the mother of all of us and the mother of each of us. She leads each of us to Jesus and helps us to be more closely united with him.

Through this book, we believe, Mary wants to help you to come closer to the Lord. She wants to teach you to pray better, and to help you to receive new outpourings of grace.

Praying With and Through Mary

This book contains material for daily personal prayer in five chapters.

Set aside some part of your day for a quiet time with the Lord. Perhaps you already do this; if you do, do not change the time you spend, but try to follow the prayer program of the book day by day. In case you do not have a regular daily time for personal prayer, decide now what time you want to set aside daily for the Lord, how much time, and when. For those who do not have a regular time, we suggest between twenty and thirty minutes, but at least fifteen minutes.

When should you pray every day? Find a time when you can be quiet and uninterrupted, for example, before others in your house get out of bed, or after they go to bed at night. Or you might choose your lunch hour, or perhaps before or after the Eucharistic Celebration, if you participate in daily Eucharist. Try to be faithful to the time. If you miss it because of something that comes up, then try to make it up before you go to bed at night.

Where should you pray? Anywhere you can. A church or chapel is good, but not possible for everyone. A quiet room or a quiet corner of a room may do. Some people can pray going to work on the bus or train. Let the Lord guide you to find a time and a place. Ask him for guidance, through the intercession of Mary.

In the following chapters, you will find help for daily prayer according to this general plan:

1. Call to mind the presence of the Lord to you, and that of his mother, Mary.

2. Read the indicated Bible text slowly and prayerfully.

3. Ask Mary to pray for you for the grace that you want which will be indicated in the *Ask for God's grace*. Then go with her to Jesus, and ask him for this grace.

4. Read the *Prayer points,* and pick out something that strikes you. Then stay with the Lord in the framework of

that point, pondering it, speaking to Jesus
words, or simply being in his presence.

5. The *Closing prayer* can be used to conclude your prayer
    time each day, or you could use it for the main part of
    your prayer, reading it as slowly as possible and stop-
    ping after a few words or a phrase. You could use those
    words or that phrase to relate to the Lord, to be with him,
    to stay united with him, and to remain quiet for a while
    in his presence.

6. When you have finished your quiet time with the Lord, read
    the *Short prayer to repeat during the day.* Place it in your
    heart. You may wish to write it on a sheet of paper and put
    it in your pocket or in your purse. You can say it frequently
    during the day, or off and on when you think of it.

How to Use This Book

This book has been written to be used by one person, but two,
three, or more can use it at the same time. If several persons
use the same book, or their own copies of the book, they have
the advantage of meeting daily or weekly for shared prayer.

If you use the book alone, you may wish to find a spiritual director, at least temporarily, or a friend that you can
share spiritually with, and meet regularly with him or her,
perhaps once a week, to share how your prayer is going. But
this is not necessary. You can schedule a time every week
when you sit down with Jesus to review the week, especially
how your prayer has been, and he will enlighten you.

The book can be prayed through over five weeks, or for as long or brief a time as it takes. Some people will find enough material for quite a long time, while others may wish to use it for a week-long or even a weekend retreat.

In any case, the prayer for any particular day need not be finished in one day or for any particular week in one week. Stay where you find the Lord, and begin the next day or the next week when you are ready.

A Few Words on Prayer

What can we do when our prayer becomes "dark," when "the lights go out"? We stay there. If this is not for reasons of sin, sickness, or suffering—nothing we can remedy—then we can say that this is the Lord's will. St. John of the Cross speaks of a "dark ray." If I see no light coming from the Lord, I can still sit there in the dark, knowing that he is there. Maybe he is even closer, and I am, as it were, in his shadow. "Where falls the sun's most radiant beam, darkest the shadow grows," says a poet quite accurately.

Consolation, an ease and joy in prayer, is a gift; darkness in prayer is equally a gift. Neither comes from our being more or less pleasing to God. During the winter, the life of a vine seems to go underground, but that is part of its preparation for fruitfulness. Stay with the Lord in the dark. Be faithful in seeking his company. He needs you, in love, just as you need him.

Gifts given to us in prayer are for service and not merely for our adornment. At the same time, the Lord takes delight in making us beautiful. He pours gifts on his beloved ones while they sleep.

> I delight greatly in the Lord;
> my soul rejoices in my God.
> For he has clothed me with
> garments of salvation
> and arrayed me
> in a robe of righteousness...
> as a bride adorns herself with jewels (Isaiah 61:10).

The Lord takes delight in us, and we delight in him more than in the gifts he gives us. It is easy to become excited when the Lord uses us, or when he comes to us in special ways in our prayer. That is fine and quite understandable. Of course, we rejoice in the Giver more than in the gifts he gives, and are more attached to him than to his gifts, however beautiful.

Thank the Lord in your prayer for the gifts he has given you in this prayer-journey and for the ways in which he is calling you even further to work with him.

Summarizing the Five Chapters

Each chapter represents a step or a phase in a process. It begins with a "reading" that, among other things, sets up the following week of prayer. The chapter continues with prayer for the following seven days, until the next "reading."

Each of the five weeks has prayer notes for every day of the week. Here is an outline of the five chapters:

1. Mary is the mother of Jesus, and she is my mother in the order of grace. All graces come to me through Mary; as mother, she nourishes me, feeds me, supports me, teaches me, and helps me to grow and to mature in the spiritual life.

2. Jesus loves me personally; he calls me by name.

3. In the light of Jesus' love for me, I realize that I have sinned, and I grasp that he, in his mercy, forgives me all my sins. Jesus' love and mercy heal the roots of sin in me.

4. Jesus is the Lord of all creation. He is my Lord, the Lord of my life and of my future. Jesus, my loving Lord, is present to me in a special way in the worship of the Church.

5. In the fifth week, Mary and Jesus help me to receive new grace, a new outpouring of the Holy Spirit. I ask to receive the Holy Spirit in a new way and in a new fullness.

Chapter I

Mary,
the Mother of Jesus
and My Mother

M ary is the mother of Jesus. Jesus is the Son of God, one person of the Divine Trinity, God. Therefore, Mary, his mother, is the Mother of God, as Christians have professed since the beginnings of Christianity. She not only *was* but *is* the Mother of God.

The relationship is permanent, for Mary was, is, and will always be his mother. Mary is the mother of Jesus, and she is my mother. All graces come to me through Mary, who is my mother in the order of grace. She nourishes me, feeds me, supports me, teaches me in her wisdom, and helps me to grow and to mature in the spiritual life.

Mary is "mediatrix of grace." She is not mediatrix in the way that Jesus, our Savior, our unique Mediator with the Father is, but Mary exercises a "maternal mediation" because she is the mother of Jesus. He came to us through her, and "Mary's motherhood continues unceasingly in the Church as the mediation which intercedes" (*Mother of the Redeemer,* n. 40).

Does this mean that I have to pray to Jesus through Mary? Not at all. It means that I *can* pray to Jesus through Mary. Mary is in no way divine; she is entirely a creature. But she is the Mother of God, the Mother of Jesus. So, I can ask her to intercede for me with Jesus, to "put in a word for me," to pray for me.

What good does it do to pray to Mary, to ask her for help, to ask her to pray for me? A great deal. At the wedding feast of Cana, would Jesus have changed the water into wine if Mary had not asked him to? He objected, and he added that the timing was wrong. But he did it because she asked him. Mary's prayer is powerful, and it can be powerful for us.

Christian tradition has always held that John stood in for each one of us when he stood with Mary at the foot of the cross, and Jesus said to John, "Behold your mother," and to Mary, "Behold your child." Mary wants to be a mother to you. She is, in fact, your mother in the spiritual order, in the order of grace.

As she is the mother of Jesus, she is mother of the life of Jesus in me, of the life of the Spirit in me. She nourishes and nurtures the divine life in me. Mary teaches me and intercedes for me. She wants to pray with me and for me: to teach me better how to pray, to bring me closer to Jesus.

PRAYER FOR THE WEEK

First Day

Mary My Mother

From the cross as he was dying, Jesus bequeathed to me his last possession: his mother. Heaven was closed; his beloved Father seemed to have turned away in his greatest hour of need: "My God, my God, why have you abandoned me?" (Mk 15:34). But Jesus' dying eyes could still see his mother standing there, so he gave her to me, in the person of John the beloved, as his dying gift: "Woman, here is your son." And Jesus bequeathed me to her: "here is your mother" (Jn 19:26–27).

Acknowledge God's presence

Say a short prayer to remind yourself that Jesus is present to you at this moment through his love for you, that Mary also is present to you through her love for you, and that you can speak to her and be with her. For example, you could say a short "thank you" prayer: "Thank you Jesus for being here with me; thank you Mary for being here with me."

Read God's Word JOHN 19:25–27

Meanwhile near the cross on which Jesus hung, his mother was standing with her sister, Mary wife of Clopas, and Mary Magdalene. Seeing his mother with the disciple whom he loved standing beside her, Jesus said to her, "Woman, this is your son"; and he said to the disciple, "This is your mother." ∼

Ask for God's grace

Ask Mary to pray for you for the day's grace, which is to know Mary better as your mother, and to know Jesus better as your Lord and Savior. Then go with Mary to Jesus and ask him for the grace that you want: to know his mother better as your mother, and to know him better.

Prayer points

Reflect on the prayer points below, taking them one at a time and beginning with whichever especially speaks to you.

1. Jesus died for me personally, to save me, as though I were the only other person who ever walked on earth. He loves me so much that he would die again if that were necessary.

2. When he was dying on the cross, Jesus gave his mother to me to be my mother. The apostle John, the disciple whom Jesus loved, stood in for me; Jesus gave her to John, Jesus gave her to me.

3. Mary is your mother who leads you to Jesus. You might wish to talk to the Lord in your own words, or you might wish to pray to Mary, at least in the beginning of your prayertime. For some or even most of the time you might just want to be silent with Jesus or Mary or both of them. Perhaps you might wish to repeat a short prayer to Mary or to Jesus, very slowly, such as, "Mary, help me to pray," or, "Thank you, Lord," or simply, "Jesus."

    In your prayer, it is important to stay in that place where you feel comfortable, where you find spiritual fruit, with whatever you feel moved to pray about. Do not hurry, but go slowly, even very slowly. If you feel at peace asking Mary to pray with you for the grace that you want, do that for a while and then move on, or do it the whole time.

Closing prayer

Mary my mother, Jesus has given you to me as my mother. Teach me to pray; help me to pray. Lead me to Jesus and help me to be with him in prayer.

Lord Jesus, thank you for dying for me. Thank you for giving me your mother. Help me to take seriously your personal love for me. Amen.

Short prayer to repeat during the day

Mary, my mother, lead me to Jesus.

The Wedding Feast at Cana

At the marriage feast at Cana, Mary's quick compassion saw the embarrassment of her hosts, the young couple whose wedding would probably become the joke of the small town as the wedding that ran out of wine. Through Mary's intercession this simple domestic situation became an enduring paradigm of her quick, unfailing access to the loving heart of her Son. She is still today, as Pope Benedict XV wrote, "absolutely incapable of refusing her help to those who invoke her" (Encyclical, *Fausto Appetente Die,* June 29, 1921).

Acknowledge God's presence

Say a short prayer to remind yourself that Jesus and Mary are present to you at this moment through his love for you, and that Mary also is present to you through her love for you, and that you can speak to her and be with her. For example, you could say a short "thank you" prayer: "Thank you Jesus for being here with me, thank you Mary for being here with me."

Read God's Word   JOHN 2:1–11

There was a wedding in the town of Cana, in Galilee. Jesus' mother was present, and Jesus and his followers were there too. They ran out of wine, and the mother of Jesus said to him, "They have no more wine." He answered her, "What is that to us? My time has not yet come." Jesus' mother said to the servants, "Do whatever he tells you." Standing near were six stone jars, the kind used for Jewish rituals of purification. Each jar could hold twenty or thirty gallons of water. Jesus told the servants, "Fill the jars with water." They filled up the jars. "Now pour some out," Jesus said, "and take it to the master of ceremonies." They did this. The master of ceremonies tasted the water, now turned into wine; he did not know where the wine came from, but the servants knew. The master of ceremonies called the bridegroom and said to him, "People serve the best wine first, and the less good wine later, when people have had more to drink; but you have kept the best wine until the last!" Jesus did this first one of his signs in Cana, in Galilee, and so he revealed his glory, and his followers believed in him. ∼

Ask for God's grace

Ask Mary to pray for you to receive the grace to know her better as your mother, and to know Jesus better. Then go with Mary to Jesus, and ask him for the grace to know his mother better as your mother, and to know him better through his love for you.

Prayer points

Slowly read the three prayer points below. Take one point to begin your prayer—and then use the others if and as you might need them. Stay where you find peace, where you find that you can relate to Mary, to Jesus, or to both of them.

1. With complete trust in Jesus, Mary asked him to solve a problem.

2. Jesus did what Mary asked, even though it did not seem the appropriate moment for him to begin his ministry by performing a miracle as a sign.

3. Jesus acted not only because his mother asked, but also out of his compassion for the bride and groom and their parents. He helped them so that they would not be embarrassed at not having enough wine for the wedding feast.

Talk to Mary, Jesus, or to both of them in your own words. Or simply be quiet in the presence of Jesus or Mary, perhaps letting the Bible text or one of the above points sink in deeper as you ponder it. You may wish to say a short prayer or the name of Jesus over and over very slowly, relating to the Lord in that way. Or you could slowly pray the closing prayer, reflecting on the words.

Stay where you feel comfortable in terms of relating to the Lord. Do not hurry, for there is no need to finish, or even to follow the points. Pray the way you feel the Lord is leading you.

Closing prayer

Mary my mother, you asked Jesus for a special favor and he
did what you asked. Ask him now for graces of prayer for
me so that I can be more united with him.

Lord Jesus, change the water of my own prayer into the
wine of *real* prayer that is content to just *be* in your presence. Give me the grace to take you seriously, knowing that
you are present to me here and looking at me with love. Amen.

Short prayer to repeat during the day

**Lord, that I may know you more clearly,
love you more dearly.**

Third Day
———

*The Angel Announces to Mary
the Good News*

Pope John Paul II says that Mary was chosen "for a
unique mission in the history of salvation: that of
being the Mother of the long-awaited Savior" (*Tertio Millen-
nio Adveniente,* n. 54). She was entirely free. She listened,
asked, and responded. "Mary, taken into dialogue with God,
gives her active consent to the Incarnation" (Pope Paul VI,
Marialis Cultus, 36 ff.). Her Son likewise discerned the will
of his Father, "Jesus Christ was not 'Yes and No,' but in him

it is always 'Yes'" (2 Cor 1:19). "Do whatever he tells you" says Mary (Jn 2:6).

Acknowledge God's presence

Remind yourself that Jesus is present to you at this moment through his love for you, and that Mary too is present through her love for you. Say, "Thank you, Jesus, for being here with me; thank you, Mary, for being here with me," or make up a short prayer of your own to increase your awareness of the presence of Mary and Jesus.

Read God's Word   LUKE 1:26–38

God sent the angel Gabriel to Nazareth, a small town in Galilee, with a message for a young woman engaged to a man named Joseph, a descendant of David. The young woman's name was Mary. The angel entered and said, "Greetings, you who have found favor with God. The Lord is with you." But she was disturbed by the greeting and wondered what it meant. The angel said to her, "Mary, do not be afraid. God gives you a great grace: you will conceive and give birth to a son, and his name will be 'Jesus.' He will be great; and he will be called 'Son of the Most High.' God will give him the throne of his ancestor David, and he will be king over Israel forever, his reign will never end." Mary said, "How can this be? I am a virgin." The angel responded, "The Holy Spirit will come upon you; the power of the Most High will overshadow you. And so the holy child to be born will be called the Son of God. What is more, your cousin Elizabeth has conceived a son in her old age, and she who was called barren is now in her sixth month because God is faithful to his promises." Mary said, "I am the handmaid of the Lord. Be it done to me as you have said." Then the angel left her. ∾

Ask for God's grace

Ask Mary to intercede for you for the grace to say "yes" to the Lord just as she did. Go with Mary to Jesus and ask him for the grace to say "yes" to him in your life and to say "yes" to his love for you.

Prayer points

Reading the three prayer points, begin where you find it easiest to relate to Mary, Jesus, or to both of them. Choose one point to begin your prayer and the others when you need them.

1. Mary said "yes" to the angel, but she really said "yes" to the Lord.

2. Mary said "yes" to having Jesus in her life. Our salvation depended on her "yes."

3. The Son of God, the second Person of the Trinity, was conceived in Mary's womb and became human like us in all things except sin.

Be with Mary, or Jesus, or both. Remain quietly with them, pondering the Bible text or one or more of the points. Remain wherever you find yourself relating easily to Mary or to Jesus.

Closing prayer

Mary, my mother, you said "yes" to God and to God's will in your life. You said "yes" to God's unconditional love for you. Help me to say "yes" to Jesus in my life and to his unconditional love for me personally.

Lord Jesus, I do say "yes" to you in my life; I say "yes" to your love for me. Thank you, Jesus. Amen.

Short prayer to repeat during the day

Yes, Jesus, yes.

Fourth Day

Mary Visits Her Cousin Elizabeth

Mary always brings Jesus to us, and Jesus always gives us his Holy Spirit. The Holy Spirit is the love of Jesus. St. Ildephonsus (607–677) prays to Mary: "I beg you, holy Virgin, that I may have Jesus from the Holy Spirit, by whom you brought Jesus forth. May my soul receive Jesus through the Holy Spirit by whom your flesh conceived Jesus.... May I love Jesus in the Holy Spirit in whom you adore Jesus as Lord, and gaze upon him as your Son."

Acknowledge God's presence

Jesus is present to you right now through his love for you, and Mary is present through her love for you. Say a short prayer to become more aware of the presence of Mary and Jesus.

Read God's Word   LUKE 1:39–56

Mary set out quickly and went into the hill country of Judah. She went into Zechariah's house and greeted Elizabeth. As soon as Elizabeth heard Mary's greeting, the child leaped in her womb, and Elizabeth was filled with the Holy Spirit. She cried aloud, and said, "Blessed are you among women, and blessed is the fruit of your womb. And who am I that the mother of my Lord comes to me? As soon as I heard the sound of your voice greeting me, the child in my womb leaped for joy. Blessed is she who has believed that the promises spoken to her by the Lord would be fulfilled."

And Mary said, "My soul magnifies the Lord, and my spirit rejoices in God my Savior. He has looked with favor on the lowliness of his handmaid. From now on, all generations will call me blessed. For the Almighty has done great things for me, and holy is his name. He shows mercy to those who fear him, from generation to generation. His strong right arm has scattered the proud in the thoughts of their hearts. He has removed the mighty from their thrones and exalted the lowly. He has filled the hungry with good things, and sent the rich away empty. He has come to the aid of his servant, Israel, remembering his mercy, according to the promise he made to our ancestors, to Abraham and to his descendants forever." And Mary stayed with her about three months, and then she returned home. ∾

Ask for God's grace

Ask Mary to obtain for you from Jesus a consciousness of his indwelling within you through the Holy Spirit. Go with Mary to Jesus to ask that you may always be aware of his presence with you.

Prayer points

1. Mary carried the unborn infant Jesus and she was filled with the Holy Spirit. Jesus lives in your heart and sends you his Holy Spirit.

   If you are able to receive the Eucharist, you could pray to prepare with Mary to receive Jesus. One of the writers of the early Church has said, "We drink the Holy Spirit from the heart of Christ." The time after Holy Communion is a privileged time for being filled with the Holy Spirit.

2. Mary's prayer of praise may provide you with prayer points. Pray the Magnificat with Mary.

3. Elizabeth was "filled with the Holy Spirit" at the visit of Mary and the unborn Jesus. Reflect that we too carry him to all whom we encounter. Speak to him now in your heart, or just rest quietly in his presence.

Closing prayer

Mary, my mother, teach me how to be always in the presence, in the company, of your Son Jesus. Guide me to be a channel of his presence to all whom I encounter.

Jesus, give me the grace to be always aware of your presence to me and in me. Amen.

Short prayer to repeat during the day

**Blessed are you among women,
and blessed is the fruit of your womb.**

Fifth Day

Mary and the Holy Spirit

From all eternity God the Father sees his own perfection and sums up his Being in one utterance: the Word. In time, "the Word became flesh and lived among us" (Jn 1:14). Jesus Christ, "is the likeness of God" (2 Cor 4:4).

He is "the image of the invisible God, the first-born of all creation" (Col 1:15). "He is the reflection of God's glory and bears the very stamp of his nature" (Heb 1:3).

Within the Trinity the Father contemplates the Son, and the Son looks at the Father. The Love that unites them is the Holy Spirit, the third Person of the Trinity. So, the Holy Spirit is Love.

Jesus Christ, God, became human to save us, to be with us. This Incarnation was accomplished by the Holy Spirit in Mary with her consent. "The Holy Spirit will come upon you" said the angel, "and the power of the Most High will cover you with its shadow. And so the child will be holy and will be called Son of God" (Lk 1:35).

For this reason Mary is sometimes called the Bride of the Holy Spirit. She is able to obtain for us the presence and the gifts of the Spirit who is God.

Acknowledge God's presence

Jesus is present to you now, and Mary is also present to you. Say a short prayer to increase your awareness of the presence of Jesus and Mary.

Read God's Word   Acts 1:14 and 2:1–4

All the apostles with one heart prayed continuously, together with some women including Mary, the mother of Jesus…. When there came the day of Pentecost, they were all together when suddenly with a great noise from heaven a violent wind filled the house they were in, and tongues of fire appeared to them over the heads of each of those present. ∼

Ask for God's grace

Ask Mary to obtain for you from Jesus an awareness of his indwelling in you through the Holy Spirit, who relates you directly to him. Go with Mary to Jesus to ask that you may always be aware of his presence with you.

Prayer points

Read the prayer points. Begin with one point and move on to the others if you have time and if the Lord leads you that way. Stay where you find you can pray.

1. Mary was present with the twelve apostles at Pentecost when the Holy Spirit descended on them all and when the Church, now filled with the Spirit, began its mission of leading all of us to union with Jesus. Besides the Twelve, Mary is the only one named in Acts, so we know that she had a special place and special role.

2. Through Mary, the Holy Spirit brings us into union with Jesus. The humble are always the first to accept Jesus: the shepherds who came to adore the newborn infant Jesus in the stable; Elizabeth when Mary visited her; Simeon and Anna in the temple who, filled with the Spirit, prayed and prophesied; and the first disciples learned to believe in Jesus at the wedding feast of Cana.

3. Filled with the Holy Spirit, Jesus' mother Mary, in and through her flesh, makes the Word of God visible. Just as God came to Moses in the burning bush and was visible as fire, so too, Jesus has come to us in and through Mary; and has been made visible in his humanity through her flesh. He comes to us through her.

Closing prayer

Mary, my mother, Jesus is with me, relating me to himself, through the Holy Spirit, Love, who brings me into close union with him. Help me to be always aware of the presence of your Son Jesus.

Jesus, you are always here with me, loving me. Give me the grace to realize that you are with me always. Amen.

Short prayer to repeat during the day

Stay with me, Lord Jesus.

Sixth Day

Mary Appears for Our Sake

In 1858, the Blessed Virgin Mary appeared eighteen times to Bernadette Soubirous, a young woman in Lourdes, southern France. The local bishop approved these apparitions in 1862.

In 1917, in Fatima, Portugal, Mary appeared six times to three children: Lucia, Jacinta, and Francisco. The local bishop approved the apparitions in 1930.

More recently, Mary has spoken to Sister Agnes Katsuko Sasagawa, who was in her early forties when the visitations began in Akita, Japan. These were approved in a pastoral letter from the local bishop in 1984.

Mary has also appeared to a woman in Betania, Venezuela. Maria Esperanza Bianchini began seeing the mother of Jesus and speaking with her in 1976; these apparitions received approval in 1987.

In Africa, several young women and one young man had a long series of visits from Mary at Kibeho in Rwanda-Burundi, beginning in 1981. The apparitions lasted a few years, and were approved by the local bishop in 1988.

In Medjugorje, an ethnically Croatian village in Bosnia-Herzogovina, Mary began appearing and speaking to several young people in the early summer of 1981. These apparitions have continued on a daily basis. In 1990, the Third Commission of Investigation, appointed by the bishops of the former Yugoslavia, approved the apparitions and recommended pastoral help for pilgrims to Medjugorje. However, the local bishop has not approved the apparitions.

Acknowledge God's presence

Jesus and Mary are present to you now. Say a short prayer to remind you of their presence.

Read God's Word   MARK 1:2–3

It is written in the book of the prophet Isaiah: "Behold, I send my messenger before you, to prepare your way before you. A voice of one shouting in the desert, 'Prepare a way for the Lord, make straight paths for him.'" ∼

Ask for God's grace

Ask Mary to obtain for you from Jesus the grace to know her as your mother, as a messenger to prepare you to receive Jesus and to be close to him.

Prayer points

Begin with one of the prayer points and stay where you find help in relating to the Lord or to Mary.

1. In our time, Jesus has sent his mother to us to call us to himself.

2. He sends Mary to the poor and the humble of this world in remote places, to children, to young people in country villages, to the uneducated, to unknown people who have no prestige in the sight of others.

3. Each time Mary has appeared, she has met the person or persons on the terms they could understand. To Bernadette of Lourdes, Mary appeared as a young country woman of southern France. She spoke French *patois* with Bernadette's own local accent. In the apparition at Fatima,

Mary was dressed as a young Portuguese woman and spoke in the children's own dialect. When she appeared in 1531 to Juan Diego as Our Lady of Guadalupe, Mary showed herself as a young, pregnant Aztec woman, in the dress of that time and place. She spoke not the Spanish of the conquering armies and of the missionaries, but the local Indian language. She affectionately called him by name, using the diminutive *Juan Dieguito,* although he was fifty-seven years old. Mary spoke as his mother; she does the same now.

Closing prayer

Mary, my mother, thank you for being God's messenger, for showing yourself to us in many ways, wearing many faces so like our own. Mary, help me to receive in my heart the message you bring from God and to live it in my life.

Jesus, thank you for giving me your loving Mother. She shows me the path to you, and walks beside me with you. I am never alone. Amen.

Short prayer to repeat during the day

Stay with me, Mary. Lead me to Jesus.

Seventh Day
_____

Mary Calls Us

In her apparitions during this century, Mary's message has been essentially the same. She brings us the same message from Jesus: (1) Conversion: turn to Jesus; (2) Faith: have faith in Jesus; (3) Prayer: pray, pray, pray.

Acknowledge God's presence

Mary has come to you and is present now, calling you to God.

Read God's Word   ISAIAH 44:21–22

I fashioned you, and you are in my service.
I will not forget you.
I have swept away your transgressions
like a cloud,
And your sins like a mist;
Come back to me, for I have redeemed you. ∽

Ask for God's grace

Ask Mary to obtain for you from Jesus the grace of a true conversion away from all sin and toward Jesus, of a deeper faith in him, and of prayer.

Prayer points

Read the prayer points. It might be better to begin today's reflections with the first point, moving on as the Lord leads you to the second and the third. Do not hurry. If the first point is enough for your prayer, then stay there the whole time.

1. Conversion away from sin and toward Jesus: "The Lord says this, 'Come back to me with all your heart, fasting, weeping, being sorry'" (Jl 2:12). "God himself has reconciled us to himself through Christ, and he has given us the work of handing on that reconciliation" (2 Cor 5:18).

2. Faith in Jesus: "With a great cloud of witnesses all around us, we too should throw off every single thing that weighs us down including the sins that cling closely to us. And with perseverance we must keep on running the race along the course that lies ahead of us. Let us keep our eyes fixed on Jesus who leads us in our faith, and who makes it what it should be" (Heb 12:1).

3. Prayer: "We do not know how to pray as we ought to pray, but the Spirit personally makes our prayer for us..." (Rom 8:26).

Closing prayer

Mary, my mother, thank you for calling me to conversion away from sin and toward Jesus, to faith in him, and to prayer.

Jesus, through the intercession of Mary, your mother, grant me a greater share of the graces of conversion, faith, and prayer. Amen.

Short prayer to repeat during the day

Jesus, help me to do whatever you tell me.

Chapter II

The Lord's Love for Me

What kind of a person is Jesus? From the Gospels we can see that he is a loving person. They tell us that a week before his crucifixion, Jesus rode into Jerusalem on a donkey and the people went wild. They cut branches off trees and waved them in the air, shouting; they made a carpet of honor by taking off their coats and throwing them on the road for the donkey to walk on. They yelled out, "Hosanna, Hosanna to the Son of David." The Jerusalem crowd went crazy with excitement when Jesus rode into town.

The religious leaders told Jesus to quiet the mob, to calm them down because they were completely out of hand. But Jesus answered that if he did quiet them, the rocks and stones in the road would begin to yell and shout.

Why did the people go wild over Jesus? Because of the kind of man he was and is—loving. Jesus has a heart full of love. At the same time, that heart full of love is gentle and humble. It calls each one of us and says, "Come to me, all you who struggle and who are weighed down, and I will make things easy for you." He adds, "Put on my yoke and learn from me."

The image is of two oxen pulling a load together. Jesus wants you to team up with him, like two oxen who pull the same cart, yoked together. He says that he will teach you how to do it. When two oxen work together, the stronger one is always a little ahead, taking the strain of the load. When you team up with Jesus, everything will go easier and better because he will be with you. He loves you personally and calls you by name. Take him seriously.

PRAYER FOR THE WEEK

First Day
———

Jesus Loves Me

How does Jesus love me? Personally. He knows me by name and he knows me perfectly: my past, present and future; all my good and bad points. Jesus' love for me does not depend on my meriting or deserving it. "I have called you by name, you are mine" (Ex 33:17). I am his, so he loves me with a love that "surpasses knowledge" (cf. Eph 3:19). His love will never let me go, for nothing can ever separate me from his love (cf. Rom 8:35).

Acknowledge God's presence

Acknowledge the loving presence of Jesus and Mary.

Read God's Word   Psalm 139

> Lord, you search me and you know me.
> You know if I am standing or sitting.
> You understand my thoughts from far away

Whether I walk or lie down,
you are watching me.
You are familiar with all my ways.
Before a word is on my tongue, Lord,
you know it completely.
Behind me and in front of me you hem me in.
You shield me with your hand.
This knowledge is beyond my understanding,
too high for me.

Where could I go to escape your gaze?
Where could I flee from your spirit?
If I climb to the heavens, you are there;
if I go down to Sheol you are there too.
If I were to fly to the point where the sun rises,
or far across the sea,
your hand would still guide me,
your right hand holding me.
If I asked darkness to cover me
and light to become night around me,
that darkness would not be dark to you;
the night would shine like the day.

You have created my inmost being;
you knit me together in my mother's womb.
For all these mysteries—
for the wonder of myself,
for the wonder of your works—
I thank you.

You know me through and through;
you watched my bones take shape
when I was being formed in secret,
woven together in the womb.
You have seen everything I have done;
all my actions have been recorded in your book.
You determined my days
before even the first one began.
Lord, your thoughts are mysterious,
infinite in scope.
I could no more count them
than I could count the sand!
And even if I could,
you would still be with me…

Lord, search me and know my heart;
make sure I do not follow evil ways,
and guide me in the way of life eternal. ∾

Ask for God's grace

Ask for the grace to grow every day in comprehending the great love Jesus has for you.

Prayer points

1. Reread Psalm 139, praying it and letting it sink in to your heart.

2. Go back and pray through it again.

3. Finally, go back to anything in it that especially struck you and stay with that for the rest of your prayer time. The point is to be with the Lord, in relationship with him.

Closing prayer

Mary, my mother, pray for me and with me for the grace to know Jesus better through a deeper realization of his love for me. Help me to take Jesus' love for me seriously. Help me to know Jesus better through a greater openness to his love for me and a deeper reception of his love. Take my hand now and take me with you to Jesus.

Lord Jesus, I come to you with your mother, the mother you have given to me as my mother. Lord, you know me thoroughly and you love me without any qualifications, without any conditions. You love me just as I am at this moment. Help me to truly believe in your love for me. I ask you this through the intercession of the Blessed Virgin Mary. Amen.

Short prayer to repeat during the day

You have made me for yourself, O Lord.

Jesus Gives Me His Love and Himself

How does Jesus love me? I know that Jesus practices what he preaches, and what he preaches about love is found all through the Gospels. In the sixth chapter of Luke's Gospel, Jesus says, "Judge not, and you will not be judged." Therefore, you know that Jesus does not judge you. He says, "Condemn not, and you will not be condemned." Therefore, you know that Jesus does not condemn you. He says, "Forgive, and you will be forgiven." Therefore, you know that Jesus forgives you everything.

He goes on to say, "Give, and it will be given to you; good measure, pressed down, shaken together, running over, will be put into your lap." What does Jesus give me? His love and himself. He died on a cross for me, out of love for me.

Acknowledge God's presence

Jesus and Mary are present here now. Prayerfully recognize that they are looking on you with love.

Read God's Word   Luke 6:37–38

Be compassionate just as your Father is compassionate. Do not judge and you will not be judged; do

not condemn, and you will not be condemned; forgive, and you will be forgiven. Give, and there will be
gifts for you: full measure, shaken, pressed down, and
overflowing, will be poured into your lap, because the
standard that you use will be the same standard used
for you. ∽

Ask for God's grace

To have a better grasp of the love that Jesus has in his heart
for you.

Prayer points

1. In your prayer, you can rest quietly in the love Jesus has
   for you, or you could apply his love to the aching or sick
   areas of your life. The unknown author of the fourteenth-
   century *Book of Privy Counseling* advises: "Take the
   good gracious God just as he is, as plain as a common
   poultice, and lay him to your sick self."

2. You can use the Closing prayer below for the main part
   of your prayer, reading it slowly and relating to Jesus in
   terms of it.

3. Spend some time just being quiet with the Lord, perhaps
   slowly repeating a word or phrase from the prayer to
   avoid distractions and remain centered on the Lord Jesus.

Closing prayer

Mary, my mother, pray for me and with me for the grace to know Jesus better through a deeper realization of his love for me. Teach me to walk in his love, to rest in his love, to live in his love for me. Teach me to enter into his loving gaze, his active love for me. Take my hand now and take me with you to Jesus.

Lord Jesus, I ask you through the intercession of the Blessed Virgin Mary for the grace to share your affections and your vision, to see with your eyes. In union with your heart, may I love God our Father, Mary our mother, and all my brothers and sisters. Amen.

Short prayer to repeat during the day

**Heart of Jesus, burning with love for me,
inflame my heart with love for you.**

Third Day

Jesus Is Love

Jesus is complete and total love. With that total love he loves me more than life itself, as he proved by dying on the cross. Therefore, my life is lit up with the radiance of his love. "His banner over me [is] love" (Song 2:4 KJV). As I walk through life, even through suffering and death, I have the reassurance of the completeness of Jesus' love for me. "As the Father has loved me, so I have loved you" (Jn 15:9).

Acknowledge God's presence

Come into the presence of Jesus and Mary who are looking at you with love here and now.

Read God's Word   1 CORINTHIANS 13:4–11

Love is always patient. Love is kind. Love is never jealous. Love is not boastful or conceited. Love is never rude; it never seeks its own advantage. Love does not get irritated or hold a grudge. Love does not rejoice at wrongdoing; it rejoices in the truth. It is always ready to make allowances, to trust, to hope, and to put up with whatever comes. Love never comes to an end.

If there are prophecies, they will end. Tongues will cease, will fall silent; and if knowledge, it will be done away with. Now we know imperfectly, and we prophesy imperfectly; but once perfection comes, then all imperfections will be done away with. When I was a child, I talked like a child, I understood things as a child does, and I thought like a child; but now that I am grown, I am finished with childish ways. ∽

Ask for God's grace

The grace to understand Jesus' love for you personally.

Prayer points

1. How does Jesus love me? Paul's First Letter to the Corin-
    thians describes love in this way (the following transla-
    tion is in some ways closer to the original Greek than the
    preceding translation):

    Love is patient and kind.
    Love is not jealous or boastful.
    Love is not puffed up with pride; it is not rude.
    Love does not insist on its own way.
    Love is not irritated or resentful.
    Love takes no joy in what is wrong; it rejoices in what
       is right.
    Love puts up with everything.
    Love believes all things.
    Love hopes all things.
    Love perseveres through everything.
    Love never fails.

2. We know from the New Testament that God is love and
    that Jesus is God. If Jesus is God, and God is love, then I
    can draw the valid theological conclusion that Jesus *is*
    love. If Jesus is love, then I can substitute the word
    "Jesus" for the word "love" in the above text. This gives
    me a personality profile of Jesus insofar as his love for

me. How does Jesus love me? What is the quality of his love for me? Here is the answer:

Jesus is patient and kind.
Jesus is not jealous or boastful.
Jesus is not puffed up with pride; he is not rude.
Jesus does not insist on his own way.
Jesus is not irritated or resentful.
Jesus takes no joy in what is wrong; he rejoices in what is right.
Jesus puts up with everything.
Jesus believes all things.
Jesus hopes all things.
Jesus perseveres through everything.
Jesus never fails.

3. Spend some time being quiet with the Lord, perhaps slowly repeating a word or phrase from St. Paul's characteristics of love.

Closing prayer

Mary, my mother, I ask you to obtain for me from Jesus the grace to know him better and to enter more deeply into the love that your Son has for me.

Lord Jesus, through the intercession of the Blessed Virgin Mary, I ask you to plant deeply in my heart the knowledge and conviction of just how much and how unconditionally you love me. "Out of your infinite glory, may you give me the power through your Spirit for my hidden self to grow strong,

so that you may live in my heart through faith, so that rooted
in love and built on love, I may know your love which is beyond all knowledge" (cf. Eph 3:14–19). Amen.

Short prayer to repeat during the day

Jesus, your love never ends.

Fourth Day
―――――

Jesus' Love Is Strong in Weakness

Jesus loves me in an entirely spontaneous way—he
just cannot help it. Somehow, he wrapped me in his
heartstrings from the moment he had the idea of creating me.
True, he does not love some of the things I do or the atti-
tudes I have, but even if I were in the "blackest" sin, he would
not stop loving me or love me less. Job said of the Lord,
"Even though he slay me, yet I will trust in him" (Job 13:15).
Jesus can sadly say to me from the cross, "Even if you slay
me, yet I will love you." But because I have sinned, I am
exactly the one his love is seeking.

Acknowledge God's presence

Recognize anew the presence of Jesus and Mary here with
you now.

Read God's Word   MATTHEW 9:10–13

When Jesus was eating in the house, many tax collectors and sinners were eating with him and his disciples. When the Pharisees saw this, they said to his disciples, "Why does your teacher eat with tax collectors and sinners?" When he heard that, Jesus said, "Those who are well do not need the doctor, but those who are sick do. Go learn what this means, 'What I want is mercy, and not sacrifice.' I came to call not the righteous people, but sinners." ⁓

2 CORINTHIANS 12:9

But he said to me, "My grace is enough for you, because my power is made perfect in weakness." I will quite gladly boast of my weaknesses, that the power of Christ may rest upon me. ⁓

Ask for God's grace

To be convinced that the love the Lord has for you does not depend on your worthiness, but on his choice. "God's choice prevails—not human merit, but his call" (Rom 9:11–12),

Prayer points

1. "I came to call not the righteous people, but sinners." How does Jesus love me? He loves me not in spite of my weakness and sinfulness, of my dark side, of that part of

myself that I reject and do not like, but partly because of it. He came to save not the just, but sinners. All of my weakness, my sinfulness, and my dark side are the opening for Jesus' compassion, which is an integral component of his love for me. My weakness and sinfulness provide a door for the merciful love of Jesus. If I were different, he would not love me the same way. He could not love me more than he does now, because he loves me infinitely.

2. On the other hand, I may not like myself and may even have a bad or inadequate self-image. I may look down on and reject a part of myself such as past sins, my character, my physical appearance, or certain personal qualities. I may wish I had the qualities I lack. But Jesus is not me; he is a person in his own right, with his own ideas, including his ideas about me. I must avoid projecting my ideas and feelings about myself onto Jesus. His sentiments are independent of what I think or how I feel about myself, and he loves me.

    So, with St. Paul, I can glory in my weakness and boast of my infirmities (cf. 2 Cor 11:30), because the power of Jesus' love for me is made perfect in my very weakness (cf. 2 Cor 12:9).

3. I want to be with the Lord just as I am, letting him shine the light of his love on me and on my life so that his love may gradually manifest itself in my frailty. I will be content with any weakness he wants to leave me with.

Closing prayer

Mary, my mother, in your Magnificat you acknowledged your lowly state: "He has looked upon the lowliness of his servant." Yet, at the same time you rejoiced because "the Almighty has done great things for me." Please ask Jesus for that grace for me—to be humbly happy and confident in his love for me despite my continued weakness and sinfulness. Help me always to return to him when I fall.

Lord Jesus, through the intercession of Mary, Mother of God and the most wonderful of creatures, let me always hold onto the truth of your love for me. Please give me the confidence that your power can operate perfectly in my weakness. Amen.

Short prayer to repeat during the day

Thank you, Jesus, for loving me.

Fifth Day
_____

Where Your Treasure Is

I am Jesus' treasure. He gave up everything, even his life, to grasp me. I can hear him saying to me figuratively: "I gave Egypt as your ransom, Ethiopia and Seba in exchange for you. Because you are precious in my sight and honored, and I love you" (Is 43:4, 5). On Calvary Jesus gave his life in exchange for me. "God proves his love for us in that while we were sinners still, Christ died for us" (Rom 5:8). I am precious in his sight, even as a sinner.

Acknowledge God's presence

Open yourself to the presence of Jesus and Mary here with you now.

Read God's Word   MATTHEW 13:44

> The kingdom of heaven is like a treasure hidden in a field, which a man found and covered up; then in his joy he goes and sells all that he has and buys that field. ∼

JOHN 15:13

> Jesus said, "You cannot have any greater love than to lay down your life for your friends." ∼

Ask for God's grace

Ask the Lord to help you to know where your treasure is to be found, and to safeguard that treasure with all your strength.

Prayer points

1. In his parables about the kingdom of heaven, Jesus teaches me what I should seek, what I should give up to obtain everything . For example, he says, "The kingdom

of heaven is like a treasure hidden in a field, which a man found and hid again; then in his joy he goes and sells all that he has and buys that field" (Mt 13:44).

For me this treasure hidden in the field is the kingdom of heaven. What is the treasure for Jesus? What is it that Jesus gave up everything for? Me!

2. Jesus gave up everything for me. I am the treasure hidden in the field for Jesus. For me he laid aside his divinity to become human: "Christ Jesus, who, though he was in the form of God, did not regard equality with God as something to be exploited, but emptied himself, taking the form of a servant, being born in human likeness. And having taken human form, he became humbler yet and obedient to the point of death, even death on a cross" (Phil 2:6–8). In his sufferings to save me, he was brought so low that, in the words of the Psalmist, Jesus could say: "Here I am now, more worm than human" (Ps 22:6). Jesus would stop at nothing to win that treasure on which he has set his heart: me.

3. He died for me on the cross as if I were the only other person that ever walked on earth. He died for me personally, individually, and he would do it again if it were necessary. No one made him do it; he did it for love of me. He said, "Greater love than this no one has, that he lay down his life for his friends" (Jn 15:13). "This has taught us love—that he gave up his life for us" (1 Jn 3:16).

Closing prayer

Mary, my mother, Jesus taught that where my treasure is, there will my heart be. Please obtain for me a constant remembrance of Jesus throughout the day.

Lord Jesus, through the intercession of the Blessed Virgin Mary, may I be single-hearted in seeking you, my treasure, and finding you in my daily circumstances, and in my heart. Amen.

Short prayer to repeat during the day

You are my treasure, Jesus.

Sixth Day

The Hidden Mystery

Paul writes of "the revelation of the mystery that was kept secret for long ages but is now made known" (Rom 16:25–26). What is this mystery? What are "the riches of the glory of this mystery"? "It is Christ in you, the hope of glory" (Col 1:27).

Acknowledge God's presence

Jesus and Mary are here with you now; prayerfully acknowledge their loving presence.

Read God's Word   Colossians 2:2–3

It is all to bind you together in love and to stir your minds, so that your understanding may come to full development, until you really know God's secret in which all the jewels of wisdom and knowledge are hidden. ∼

Ask for God's grace

To enter into the wonderful mystery of Christ's dwelling in you in love.

Prayer points

1. St. Paul wrote to the first Christians at Colossae to tell them of a responsibility God had given him. He said that this responsibility was a message—God's message, hidden until then, but now revealed—a mystery rich in glory.

    "God has made me responsible for delivering his message to you. The message is a mystery that was hidden for generations and centuries. It has now been revealed. God wanted it to be revealed to show all its rich glory. The mystery is Christ in you, the hope of glory. This is the Christ we proclaim. This is the wisdom that we try to teach everyone" (Col 1:25–28).

2. Christ lives in me; this is the mystery rich in glory. This is the wisdom in my life, the center from which I operate, or rather, from which Jesus wants to operate. "I live

now not with my own life but with the life of Christ who lives in me" (Gal 2:20). "For me, to live is Christ" (Phil 1:21).

3. "We hold this treasure in earthenware jars" says St. Paul (2 Cor 4:7). We are fragile, but it is "so that the greatness of the power is God's, and not ours."

Closing prayer

Mary, Mother of Jesus, you know all the wonders of God's plan though even for you, "It is impossible to fathom the marvels of the Lord" (Sir 18:6). Please thank Jesus with me for the wonders of his love.

Jesus, thank you. One day I will see you face to face. Until then, may I "live out the time of my exile here in reverent awe" at the wonders of your love and plans for me (cf. 1 Pet 1:17). Amen.

Short prayer to repeat during the day

How wonderful your love, O Lord!

The Wonders of His Love

C hrist in me—the hidden mystery now revealed—is my treasure. He is "the reflection of God's glory and the exact imprint of God's very being" (Heb 1:3). Jesus is "the image of the invisible God" (Col 1:15). In prayer, I can just be in that presence. I don't need to *do* anything but just to be there in that glory. "God...has shone in our hearts to give the light of the knowledge of the glory of God in the face of Jesus Christ" (2 Cor 4:6–8).

Acknowledge God's presence

Jesus and Mary are here with you now and looking at you with love; acknowledge their presence.

Read God's Word   2 Corinthians 3:18

Our unveiled faces reflect like mirrors the brightness of the Lord, and they all grow brighter and brighter as we turn into the image that we reflect. This is the work of the Lord who is Spirit. ∿

Ask for God's grace

Ask Jesus that you may better understand his great love for you and respond to it more faithfully.

Prayer points

1. In your prayer you may wish to remain silently before the Lord gazing at him as if with "unveiled face." Because we are blind, we can gaze fully on his glory.

2. Jesus lives in us, but, even more, he makes us sharers in his divine nature. During the Eucharistic celebration as the priest puts a small drop of water into the chalice of wine, he prays: "By the mystery of this water and wine may we come to share in the divinity of Christ, who humbled himself to share in our humanity." We do not become God, but we are caught up into God by the Holy Spirit in our hearts. By grace we are "divinized."

3. One could consider that others also share the wonder of his indwelling. Do I treat everyone with respect? Do I treat myself as God's dwelling? "Did you not know that you are God's temple and that the Spirit of God lives in you? If anyone should destroy the temple of God, God will destroy him, because the temple of God is sacred, and you are that temple" (1 Cor 3:16–17).

Closing prayer

Mary, my mother, "the love of Christ overwhelms me" (cf. 2 Cor 5:14). Teach me how to love Jesus as generously as I can. You know how much Love longs to be loved.

Jesus, thank you for the wonders of your love. I give you my whole heart. I ask to love you above all, and to love with you all those whom you have given to me as gifts of your love. Amen.

Short prayer to repeat during the day

Thank you, Jesus, for loving me. I love you.

Chapter III

My Sin
and the Mercy
of the Lord

This week of prayer concerns sin and forgiveness. I have sinned, but I am a forgiven sinner. I can accept the Lord's forgiveness only to the extent that I realize I need it, that I have sinned and need the Lord's forgiveness.

What is sin? What is the nature of my sinfulness, of my sins? There are three ways of looking at sin.

1. I can consider each sin as breaking God's law. In this case, my sorrow for sin consists in fear of punishment. Small children have this attitude of fear when they have done something wrong. They are afraid of being caught and punished for what they have done, because they have an immature conscience.

2. I can understand sin as something bad for me, which goes against my own personal growth and diminishes me. By sinning I may hurt other people and, in some way, I always hurt myself. In this second case, I am sorry for my sins because I have hurt myself and I have gone against my best interests. This is a somewhat mature conscience.

3. I can see sin for what it really is: a refusal of the Lord's personal love for me. I am sorry because I have refused the Lord's love. I have offended him by turning my back on him, by rejecting him at least temporarily. The gratifi-

cation of my own needs and impulses were more important to me than the Lord, at least at that moment. In this
case, I have a mature conscience.

The problem, however, is not just sin, but sinfulness. I
have a tendency to sin, and I live in a world affected by sin.
Even the political, economic, and social structures of the
world around me have been infected by sin. I am a person
who sins in a world that sins.

Sin alienates and separates me from God. Jesus saves
me from this separation and this alienation by his love for
me that led him even to lay down his life to save me. He
forgives my sins and he redeems my sinfulness.

I want to recognize my sins and my sinfulness, and to
accept his forgiveness. I want the power of the mercy of Jesus
to heal me of my sinfulness and of my sinful tendencies.

PRAYER FOR THE WEEK

First Day
_____

Recognizing and Renouncing My Sinfulness

S in is always a choosing of my own selfish desires or passions over the love of God. I put myself first, and mentally justify what I plan to do.

Acknowledge God's presence

Say a short prayer to remind yourself that Jesus and Mary are with you, looking at you with love.

Read God's Word   LUKE 15:11–20

Jesus said, "A man had two sons. The younger son said to his father, 'Father, give me now my inheritance, my share of your money and goods, the part that would come to me when you die.' So, the father gave it to him. A few days later, the younger son got his things together and left for a faraway place where he wasted all his money living a bad life. When he had used up everything he had, that country had a severe shortage of food. Hungry, he found a job on a local farm feeding the pigs. And he would have been glad to eat the husks that the pigs ate, but that was not permitted. Finally he came to his senses and said to himself, 'the men who work on my father's farm have all the food they want, and more; and here I am dying of hunger. I will get out of here, and go back to my father, and say, 'Father, I have sinned against heaven and against you; I do not deserve any more to be called your son, but please take me on as a worker.' So, he left that place and went back to his father." ∿

Ask for God's grace

Ask Mary to pray with you for the grace that you want: to be aware of your sins and your sinfulness, to renounce them, and to return more completely to the Lord. Then go with Mary to Jesus, and ask him for the same grace.

Prayer points

Take the prayer points below and pray about them one at a time, beginning with the first.

1. The younger son came to his senses. He became conscious of what he had done, of his sins, and he was aware of his miserable situation. Ask the Lord for the grace to

be more aware of your sinfulness and of your sins, but do not make an examination of conscience. Rather, stay in the light of Jesus' love for you, and let the light of his love illuminate you. Let the light of his love into the dark places within you to show you more clearly your sins and your sinfulness. When seen with the Lord's eyes, as it were, your sins and sinfulness may be different than what you think.

2. The prodigal son renounced his condition, and went back to his father. Renounce your sins. Renounce the gratification of your sinful impulses and tendencies, and turn to Jesus.

3. The young man returned to his father. Jesus says this to you: "Come back to me, with all your heart." Return to the Lord your God, because he is forgiving and compassionate, slow to get angry, and rich in mercy (cf. Jl 2:12–13).

Closing prayer

Mary, my mother, pray for me that I might be more aware of my sins and my sinfulness. Help me to renounce my sins and sinful tendencies and to turn more completely to Jesus.

Lord Jesus, I come to you with the mother whom you have given to me. I ask you for the grace to be more conscious of my sinfulness and of my sins. Let me feel their weight and ugliness. Give me the grace to renounce my sins and my sinfulness, and to turn to you and to your merciful love for me. Amen.

Short prayer to repeat during the day

Thank you, Jesus, for your forgiving love.

Repenting and Accepting Forgiveness

I n the parable of the Prodigal Son, the younger boy in his misery and need set out to return to his father. He felt more sorry for himself than for his offense against his loving father. Without realizing it, he intended to bargain: "Make me one of your hired servants." In other words: "I will make up for my offense by working—I will earn my way." He had sorrow, but only a limited sorrow. The total love with which his father reached out to his returning son was the catalyst that caused his bargaining attitude to fall away and to leave a deep, needy acceptance of overwhelming love, in a spirit of true sorrow.

Acknowledge God's presence

Mary and Jesus are here. Turn to them in prayer.

Read God's Word   Luke 15:20–24

   While the younger son was still a long way down
the road from his father, his father saw him and was
filled with compassion. The father ran to his son, put
his arms around him, and kissed him. His son said,
"Father, I have sinned against heaven and against you.
I do not deserve to be called your son any more." The
father said to his servants, "Quick! Bring out the best
robe and put it on him. And get the fattened calf and
kill it. And let us eat and celebrate. This son of mine
has been dead, and now he is alive; he's been lost, and
now he's found." And the celebrations began. ∽

Ask for God's grace

Ask Mary to pray with you for the grace to repent of your
sins and of your sinful tendencies and impulses, of all your
sinfulness, and to accept the Lord's healing forgiveness and
merciful love. Ask Jesus, through Mary's intercession, for
those same graces.

Prayer points

1. The father ran to his son, put his arms around him, and
   kissed him. He did all this before the son said he was
   sorry, and while he was still in his filthy clothes, starv-
   ing, and disgraced. The knowledge of Jesus' mercy and
   compassionate love for you permits and encourages you

to be sorry for your sins, even to run to him in incomplete sorrow.

2. The younger son said to his father, "Father, I have sinned against heaven and against you." Say this to Jesus: "Jesus, I have sinned against heaven and against you." Repent and express sorrow to Jesus for your sins or at least tell him you want to be truly sorry.

3. The father said to his servants, "Quick! Bring out the best robe and put it on him. Get the fattened calf and kill it. Let us eat and celebrate, for this son of mine has been dead, and now he is alive; he's been lost, and now he's found." Accept the merciful, forgiving, and healing embrace of Jesus. Let him put his arms around you in mercy. As the father rejoiced in the return of his son, Jesus rejoices in your repentance. Rejoice with him and be happy to have received complete forgiveness.

    "There is more joy in heaven," Jesus said, "over one returning sinner, than over ninety-nine just."

Closing prayer

Mary, my mother, please pray for me and with me now for the grace of sincere repentance for all my sinfulness and for all my sins. Help me to accept the merciful and forgiving love of Jesus that washes my sins away and heals my sinfulness.

Lord Jesus, I am sorry for all my sinfulness and for all my sins. Help me to accept your merciful and forgiving love and the healing power of your embrace. Jesus, thank you for taking delight in forgiving me. Give me the grace to rejoice with you in your forgiveness, to rejoice in being a forgiven sinner and to be with you. Amen.

Short prayer to repeat during the day

Lord, thank you for your forgiving love.

Forgiving and Accepting Forgiveness

One can feel sympathy for the dutiful older son in the Prodigal Son parable, because he had never given his father cause for anxiety, yet seemed to receive less. But, the younger boy most resembled their father. Both the father and younger son were prodigal: one in giving, one in spending. Both were free of convention; both were loving, giving, and accepting. Because the older boy was tight-fisted and restricted, he felt resentful and jealous. He did not realize his father's love for him and so was not free to be forgiving.

Acknowledge God's presence

Mary and Jesus are with you. Acknowledge their presence.

Read God's Word   LUKE 15:25–32

The older son was in the fields; on his way back to the house, he heard music and dancing. He asked one of the workers what was going on. The worker answered, "Your brother has come home, and your father has had the fattened calf killed because your brother has come back safe and sound." The older son got angry, and he would not go into the house. His father came out of the house and begged the older son to come in. He talked back to his father, "Listen to me. All these years I've worked like a slave for you, and I've never once disobeyed you. And you never gave me even a young goat so that I could have a party with my friends. And here comes this son of yours. He's eaten up all your property and your belongings, he and his prostitutes, and you kill the calf we have been fattening." The father said, "Son, you're with me all the time, and everything that I have is yours. But we had to rejoice and have a party, because this brother of yours was dead and has come back to life. He was lost, and he has been found." ∿

Ask for God's grace

Ask Mary to pray that you receive the grace to forgive those who have hurt you willingly or without knowing it, especially those who have hurt you the most. Ask for the grace to accept again the Lord's forgiveness. Let Mary take your hand and lead you to Jesus. Ask Jesus for these same graces.

Prayer points

See if the first point applies to you. Take a good look, and if it does not, go on to the second point. If you have time and the Lord so leads you, proceed to the third point.

1. The older son was in the fields and on his way back to the house, he heard music and dancing. He became angry with his father and would not go into the house. It is possible to be angry with God. Am I angry with God? If so, I have to forgive him not because he has done anything wrong, but because I am perhaps wrongly but nonetheless really angry with God. God is infinitely great, big enough to accept my anger without any problem, and big enough to fully forgive me.

2. We can suppose that the older son forgave not only his father but also his brother. One could say that the older boy was justly angry on behalf of his father whose life-long earnings had been squandered by his profligate son. But his words, "you never gave me a young goat even to party with my friends," betray his true hurt. He feels less loved than his younger brother. I too need to forgive those who have hurt me, whether or not they intended to. If I retain some lack of forgiveness in my heart, then to that extent my heart is closed. If I close my heart to even one

person, then I close it to all people and to the Lord. If my heart is closed, the Lord's forgiveness cannot fully enter my heart. I wear a shield around my heart, blocking the entrance of the Lord's mercy. I need to forgive, over and over, even up to seventy times seventy, so as to have an open heart and receive the Lord's loving forgiveness.

Ask him now: Whom do I need to forgive? Who has hurt me the most? Usually I am most hurt by someone I have trusted to love me; I have been and perhaps still am vulnerable to that person, and so that person can really hurt me. Sometimes I need to forgive someone who has acted violently toward me, whether physically, psychologically, or verbally. I may also need to forgive myself, whether for some serious sin in my past or for some fault I have now.

3. I can accept the Lord's mercy again, now that I have exercised forgiveness and opened my heart more to his forgiveness and compassion toward me. I can be happy with him, because he is happy to forgive me. He rejoices in my acceptance of his forgiveness. I can rejoice, too. I have sinned, but I am forgiven.

Closing prayer

Mary, my mother, thank you for praying with me and for me for the grace to forgive. I ask you to pray with me for the grace of an always more forgiving and compassionate heart.

Lord Jesus, I do forgive those who in any way have caused me pain or hurt. And I accept your loving forgiveness of all my sins, especially the worst, and of all my sinfulness. Amen.

Short prayer to repeat during the day

Lord, forgive me. I forgive....

Fourth Day

Receiving Forgiveness for the Sins of My Life

If we were to ask the Lord about our past sins, he would not know what we meant, for when the Lord forgives he does so utterly. "You have thrown all my sins behind your back" (Is 38:17). The Lord insists that his complete forgiveness of us and his absolute blotting out of our sins, however heinous, are as much for his sake, in love, as for ours: "I am he who blots out your transgressions for my own sake, and I will not remember your sins" (Is 43:25). We need to take up the Lord's promise, and not hold on to guilt. Our sin only makes him love us more.

Acknowledge God's presence

Mary and Jesus are with you. Recognize them here present with you now.

Read God's Word   Psalm 69:13–14, 18, 29–30

> I make my prayer to you, O Lord,
> now in this time of your grace.
> Answer me with your help that never fails.
> In the kindness of your love, in your compassion,
>   answer me.
> Rescue me from the swamp; let me not sink any more.
> Come to me and ransom my life, redeem me.
> I suffer. I am in pain.
> Protect me with your saving support.
> I will praise your name in song.
> I will give you glory by thanking you. ∼

Ask for God's grace

Ask Mary to pray with you for the grace to be sorry for the sins of your whole life, and to open your heart to the Lord's mercy and his forgiveness of those sins.

Prayer points

Take these points in order.

1. Divide your life into stages: the first stage could be early childhood until ten years old; the second pre-adolescence and early adolescence, and so on. Don't create too many stages; three or four should be enough.

2. For each time frame in your life: (a) Let Jesus reveal to you, in the light of his love for you, what sins you have committed, where you have turned your back on him, how you have "let him down"; (b) tell him you are truly sorry; (c) accept his forgiveness, and if you have already repented of these sins accept it again.

3. Conclude by thanking and praising the Lord for his mercy in your life, for his all-embracing and complete forgiveness of absolutely all your sins and sinfulness.

Closing prayer

Thank you, Mary, for being here, for praying with me, for guiding my prayer. Thank you, Jesus, for my whole life, especially for your forgiveness of even those things that I have forgotten or that I will remember only later on. Amen.

Short prayer to repeat during the day

Jesus, I accept your mercy and forgiveness.

Repentance

We have sinned, yet Jesus paid the price for us. "The Lord has laid on him the iniquity of us all" (Is 53:6). "He it is who gave himself for us that he might redeem us from all iniquity and purify for himself a people of his own who are zealous for good deeds" (Ti 2:14). Truly believing in and accepting forgiveness brings us into a new dimension of living because God "has rescued us from the power of darkness and transferred us into the kingdom of his beloved Son in whom we have redemption, the forgiveness of our sins" (Col 1:13–14). We are to "live as children of the light" (Eph 5:8), forgiven, loved.

Acknowledge God's presence

Jesus and Mary are here with you; address them briefly in prayer.

Read God's Word   PSALM 51:1–17

In accord with your steadfast love for me, Lord, and
     according to your great mercy,
have mercy on me.
Wash away all my guilt.
Clean me and free me from all sin.
I know my sinfulness,

and my sin haunts me.
Against you, you alone, have I sinned.
You have seen me do what is wrong.
You are justified in your judgment of me.
You are fair. I deserve the worst.
Yes, I was born guilty, already a sinner
when my mother conceived me in her womb.

What you want is sincerity,
honesty with myself and before you.
So, teach me wisdom in my inmost heart.
Bathe me with purifying herbs until I am clean.
Wash me until I sparkle.
Make me joyful and happy.
Let these crushed bones be glad.
Do not look at my sins.
Blot out my sinfulness.

Lord, create in me a clean heart.
Put a new spirit, a new soul, into me.
Do not drive me out of your presence
or take away from me your Holy Spirit.
Save me and revive my joy.
Strengthen and encourage my willingness.

I will teach sinners your ways,
and those who have gone astray
will return to you.
Deliver me from death, O Lord my Savior.

And I will sing about the freedom you give me.

Lord, open my lips,
and my mouth will proclaim your praise.
Sacrifices give you no pleasure.
If I offered you a holocaust,
you would not take it.
The sacrifice that you want, Lord,
is my spirit humbled before you.
You will not look away
from a humbled and contrite heart. ∾

Ask for God's grace

Ask Mary to pray with you and for you for the grace to be sorry for your sins and your sinfulness, and to accept the Lord's merciful and healing forgiveness. With Mary, ask Jesus for these same graces.

Prayer points

Take these points in order.

1. Read the verses from Psalm 51 as slowly as you can. Let them sink in as you ponder them and especially pray them. You can pray the Psalm to Jesus.

2. If there is still time when you have finished, go back to the verse or verses that struck you most.

3. End your prayer by thanking the Lord for his mercy.

Closing prayer

Make up a closing prayer in your own words, perhaps using some words, phrases, or verses from Psalm 51.

Short prayer to repeat during the day

Wash me, Lord, and I'll be clean.

Sixth Day
———

Healing the Roots of My Most Frequent Sin

R oots are notoriously difficult to eradicate, some more than others. A repeated pattern of sin indicates a troublesome root. The Lord can heal us in ways we do not comprehend, because he sees clearly. A pattern of serious, perhaps addictive sin needs a sovereign grace because the root may be beyond our reach. We can cry out to the Lord for such a life-transforming grace. He will answer our prayer in his own time and way.

Acknowledge God's presence

Jesus and Mary are here; greet them briefly in prayer.

Read God's Word PSALM 30:2–3

I cried to you for help, my God, and you healed me. You brought me back from the world of the dead. I stood with those who stand in the depths, but you have restored me to life. ∾

Ask for God's grace

Pray first to Mary and then to Jesus for the grace of interior healing, for the healing of the roots of sin, and for the healing of the roots of anything else that might keep you from a closer union with the Lord.

Prayer points

Take these points in order.

1. Ask the Lord, through Mary's prayers and help, to show you what your main sin is, the sin that lies at the root of many other sins. What is your most common sin? It could be something you often overlook, such as failure to love as much as you should, selfishness or possessiveness in loving those whom you love, lukewarmness in spiritual matters such as prayer. Or it could be something else under the heading of one of the capital sins: pride, anger, envy, greed, lust, laziness, or gluttony.

     Specifically renounce that sin in all its manifestations and in its roots.

2.   Ask Jesus to heal the sin at its very roots. Do not pray that Jesus will take away your freedom to sin, because that would limit your freedom to love. Pray that he will take any compulsion out of the temptations or tendencies you might have to that sin. Or, as the case may be, pray that he will take away any sloth or inertia from your heart so that you will not sin through omitting what he calls you to be or to do.

3.   Thank the Lord for what he has done, even if you feel nothing. He may really root out that sin, or he may weaken it to a greater or lesser degree, or he may leave you with that sinful tendency for your own greater humility, like a thorn in the flesh, that you might keep turning to him.

Closing prayer

Mary, pray with and for me to be rid of my main sin and, if possible, of that sinful tendency.

     Jesus, save me from this sin. Give me the strength and the will to avoid it in the future. Amen.

Short prayer to repeat during the day

Heal me, Lord, and I'll be healed.

Healing of Memories

Memories of past hurts cripple some people. The Lord does not want that. He has forgiven the people who hurt us—because he loves them, even in their sinfulness. "He is kind to the ungrateful and to the wicked" (Lk 6:35). Some hurts and injustices seem so unbearable as to be beyond our power to recover. We need to place those hurts into Jesus' passion. He was killed by wickedness, but was raised to *new* life. He kept the marks of his wounds, but they are glorious now. He wants this for us: "Just as Christ was raised from the dead by the Father's glory, so we too might walk in newness of life" (Rom 6:4).

Acknowledge God's presence

Jesus and Mary are here; greet them briefly in prayer.

Read God's Word   Psalm 147:3

God heals the brokenhearted and binds up all their wounds. ∼

Malachi 4:2

For you who hold my name in reverence, the sun of righteousness shall rise with healing in its wings. ∼

Ask for God's grace

Pray first to Mary and then to Jesus for the grace of the heal-ing of any painful or hurtful memories from the past that might be at the root of present-day sins or of difficulties in relating to the Lord.

Prayer points

Take these points in order.

1. Ask Jesus to walk back with you into your past, to take the hurt out of the painful memories. Jesus will not take the memory away; he will heal it by healing the hurt, pain, fear, sense of inadequacy, or negative feelings from the memory. He will shine the light of his love into the dark places of your life.

    You may need healing of memories because of a painful childhood, a less than perfect relationship with your mother or with your father when you were growing up, poverty, or one or more terrible situations in your family. Go back to that time, to those memories, and let Jesus into them; ask him to heal them. When you do, be sure to forgive in your heart anyone who has hurt you or helped to cause the pain or the problem.

    You may need healing of memories because of what you have done: a crime, a serious sin against another human being, a series of sins such as thefts, neglecting someone, or sexual sins. Go back to those sins and ask Jesus to heal you.

You may need healing of memories because of some particularly bad experience, such as violence against your person, a serious accident, getting lost, a loss through death or absence of a parent, a child, other relative, a friend, or perhaps even a pet. Let Jesus walk into that memory, take the pain and the hurt out of it, and heal that memory.

2. Take that memory or those memories and any bad things that might stem from them and put them right into Jesus' hands. Give them to him. He wants to take them; they are his problem now. Let him heal you.

3. Thank the Lord for what he has done, even if you feel nothing.

Closing prayer

Mary, pray with and for me to end this time of healing of memories with Jesus. Thank you, Jesus, for your healing love. Amen.*

Short prayer to repeat during the day

Lord, into your hands I commend my spirit.

---

* If any memories or negative feelings disturb you after this prayer, it means that the Lord has not finished his healing work. Give those memories and feelings to Jesus for healing whenever they come to the surface. You may also need to seek the help of a professional counselor or therapist to walk with you toward healing.

Chapter IV

Jesus
Is
Lord

Inner Healing

The prayer for the last two days of this past week has been for inner healing. Perhaps you did not get that far into the week. Or perhaps you did, but you feel that the Lord wants to continue to heal you. In any case, if a group is praying this theme together, this fourth session should be devoted to a group prayer for inner healing. This prayer could be led by someone with experience in group prayer for inner healing. Or the group could listen to an audio tape of such a prayer; there are many such tapes available.

If you are praying on your own, then you may or may not be finished with inner healing. You may feel you need more. You could listen to an inner healing audio tape yourself and pray along with it, stopping the tape for a while when you need more time. If you have any trouble finding such a tape, try contacting a nearby office of the Catholic Charismatic Renewal—almost all have audiotapes to sell or lend. Or you could just go back to one of the inner healing prayers in the previous week. Stay wherever you feel the Lord has not yet finished healing you.

The Lordship of Jesus

Jesus is Lord. This is, we might say, the "slogan of Christianity." *Lord* is the title most often given to Jesus in the Acts of the Apostles and in the letters of Paul.

When Jesus ascended into heaven after his resurrection, the apostles needed to call him by some kind of a title that would show his divinity and sovereignty over everyone and everything in the world and in history. Under the inspiration of the Holy Spirit, they remembered his discussion with the leaders of Israel in which he quoted Psalm 110, implying that he himself was the Messiah and the Lord referred to in that Psalm. And in fact he is; there is no doubt that Jesus understood his own identity partly in the terms of Psalm 110. He is Lord.

PRAYER FOR THE WEEK

First Day

Jesus Is Lord

Jesus invites us to friendship: "I no longer call you servants...I call you friends because I have told you everything I learned from my Father" (Jn 15:15). Yet, Jesus is Lord. We have to balance those two relationships. After his transfiguration, Jesus and the three disciples came down from the mountain and saw a crowd waiting. Some of Jesus' glory must still have been evident, for Mark 9:14 describes the crowd's reaction in words which could sum up our relationship to Jesus our friend and Lord: "They were filled with awe, and they ran to meet him."

Acknowledge God's presence

Say a short prayer to remind yourself that Jesus and Mary are here with you now in your prayer time, both looking at you with love.

Read God's Word   MARK 12:35–37

Teaching in the temple, Jesus said, "How can the scribes say that the messiah is the son of David? Because David himself, moved by the Holy Spirit, said,

"'The Lord said to my Lord,

Sit at my right hand

while I make your enemies a footstool for you.'"

"David himself calls the messiah 'Lord,' so how can the messiah be the son of David?" And the crowds listened to Jesus with delight. ∽

Ask for God's grace

Ask Mary present with you to pray for the grace that you want: to know Jesus better so that you can love him more and follow him more closely. Ask Jesus for the same grace.

Prayer points

1. "The Lord said to my lord," David wrote when he composed this Psalm. The first "Lord" is God, and the second "lord" is the messiah. The problem is: how can the messiah, who should be lower than David since he is the descendant of David, be, at the same time, higher than David as his lord? We know the answer: that lord and that messiah is Jesus, truly God and truly human.

2.   Some of the scribes and the Pharisees would neither ac-
     cept Jesus as Lord nor as the Messiah who was proph-
     esied to come. You do. Tell Jesus that you accept him and
     profess him as Lord and as Savior (that is, as Messiah).

3.   Jesus, the Lord of all things in heaven and on earth, over
     everything and everyone, is here now with you, loving
     you and calling you to be with him, to know him better,
     to love him more, to follow him.

Closing prayer

Mary my mother, mother of my Lord, the Lord of all, help
me to always accept and to profess Jesus as my personal Lord
and Savior.

Lord Jesus, you are my Lord and the Lord of everything.
Teach me to know you better, to love you more, and to follow you more closely. Amen.

Short prayer to repeat during the day

Jesus, you are Lord.

Second Day

Jesus Is Lord of All Things

To know Jesus as Lord is a gift. "No one can say 'Jesus
is Lord' except by the Holy Spirit" (1 Cor 12:3). So

much depends on our knowing Jesus—our eternal life depends on it: "This is eternal life, that they may know you, the only true God, and Jesus Christ whom you have sent" (Jn 17:3). We are incapable of knowing Jesus without this gift, "No one knows the Son except the Father" (Mt 11:27).

Acknowledge God's presence

Jesus and Mary are here with you now; greet them in prayer.

Read God's Word   Colossians 1:15–18

Jesus Christ is the image of the unseen God.
In him, all things have been created,
everything in heaven and on earth:
all things, visible and invisible,
Thrones, Dominations, Sovereignties, Powers.
Before anything was created, he existed.
He is the beginning.
He was the first to be born from the dead (to rise)
so that he should be first in every way.
He is Lord. ∾

Ask for God's grace

Ask Mary here present to pray with you and for you for the grace to know Jesus better so that you can love him more and follow him more closely. Ask the same grace from Jesus himself.

Prayer points

1. "In him all things have been created." Each thing as well
    as everything is created in Jesus. The idea of this text is
    that everything that exists has its existence in and through
    the risen Jesus. He holds all things in existence. He con-
    tinuously gives them their existence. That is to say, Jesus
    is really Lord, not just because God the Father has ap-
    pointed him Lord, but because without him nothing would
    even be—including you.

2. "He was the first to be born from the dead (to rise) so that
    he should be first in every way." Jesus has gone ahead of
    each one of us into the world-to-come, creating it by his
    resurrection, and preparing a place for each of us, for you
    personally. He is Lord of heaven as well as of earth.

3. "Thrones, Dominations, Sovereignties, Powers," Jesus
    is Lord of them all. What are they? No one really knows.
    They stand for that part of reality that remains undiscov-
    ered to us, mysterious, but, nevertheless, known to Jesus
    and totally under his Lordship. I need fear nothing, not
    even what I do not know and do not understand. The
    Lord even of all that I do not understand is Jesus, my
    own Lord, and the Lord of my life.

Closing prayer

Mary my mother, mother of my Lord, the Lord of all, help
me to know Jesus better, to love him more, and to follow

him more closely. Help me to always accept and profess Jesus as my personal Lord and Savior.

Lord Jesus, you are my Lord and the Lord of everything. Teach me to know you better, to love you more, and to follow you more closely. May I always take you as my Lord and Savior. Amen.

Short prayer to repeat during the day

Lord, may I know you more clearly, love you more dearly, follow you more nearly, day by day.

Third Day

Jesus Is Lord of My Life

As Lord, Jesus could make absolute claims on my life, but he prefers the approach of friendship. Jesus is God, and as God has no need of anyone. We can give him nothing. Yet he chose to be vulnerable, to need love. "Will you also go away?" he sadly asked the Twelve when "many of his disciples walked no more with him" (Jn 6:67). He asked Peter "Do you love me?" and Peter, out of the muddle of his love, weakness, fidelity, and fear cried desperately: "Lord you know…I love you" (Jn 21:15). It is the same with us— Jesus desires my love just as I need his.

Acknowledge God's presence

Jesus and Mary are here with you now; in prayer acknowledge their presence.

Read God's Word   PHILIPPIANS 2:5–11

Have the same attitude that Jesus Christ had:
who, although he was in the divine form, God,
did not count being equal to God as
something to be held on to.

Instead, he emptied himself,
taking the form of servant,
taking human form, and being in every way
a human being
he was even more humble,
even to the acceptance of death, and even death on a
    cross.
For this reason God has raised him up
and has given him the name,
which is above all other names,
so that every single thing
in the earth, or above it, or under it,
should bend the knee at that name, the name that Jesus
    has,
and so that every tongue should acknowledge
Jesus Christ as LORD
to the glory of God the Father. ⌒

Ask for God's grace

Ask Mary here present to pray with you and for you for the grace to know Jesus better so that you can love him more and follow him more closely. Ask the same grace from Jesus himself.

Prayer points

1. "Have the same attitude that Jesus Christ had." Jesus has given us the example and he wants us to have the same attitude of loving service toward others that he had and still has toward each one of us. He did not cling to his dignity as God, did not take advantage of his rank, but humbly placed himself at the service of all. He has given us an example of love.

2. "He emptied himself." He gave himself, even to death on the cross. There is no love without suffering. Jesus loves me so much that he suffered even death on a cross for me, to save me. He is a Lord who has become like us, and even more, he died on a cross for each of us.

3. The name, which is above all other names here is not "Jesus" but "Lord." "Lord" is Jesus' proper title. In the Old and New Testaments the title, "Lord," almost always refers to God. It is a name of divinity. Jesus is God, the Son of God, and so he has the name "Lord," the highest name. He became the lowest, emptying himself, and so he has become the highest, the Lord of all.

Closing prayer

Mary my mother, mother of my Lord, the Lord of all, help me to know Jesus better, to love him more, and to follow him more closely. Help me to always accept and profess Jesus as my personal Lord and Savior.

Lord Jesus I pray together with the Blessed Virgin Mary, your mother whom you have given to me as my mother. You are Lord, the Lord God, the Lord of all things in heaven and on earth. I adore you and I thank you, because you are a loving Lord. You gave Your life for me, out of love for me. Thank you, Jesus. Amen.

Short prayer to repeat during the day

Jesus, you are the Lord of my life.

Fourth Day
———

Jesus Is a Loving Lord

Our coming to know Jesus more depends on our spending time with him. Without time together, a relationship can die. Since he is my life, without him I will wither: "Anyone who does not remain in me is thrown away like a branch—and withers" (Jn 15:6). Spending time in Jesus' company fills my life with "the fragrance that comes from knowing him" (2 Cor 2:14).

Acknowledge God's presence

In prayer, acknowledge the presence of Jesus and Mary here, looking at you with love now.

Read God's Word   Ephesians 1:3–4, 20–23

Blessed be the Father of our Lord Jesus Christ, who has blessed us with every spiritual blessing from heaven, and chosen us in Christ before the beginning of the world to be holy and without fault before him in love.

God has put his great power to work in Christ when he raised him from the dead and seated him at his right hand in heaven, far above every principality, ruler, power, and dominion, and above every name that exists now and forever. He has put all things under his feet, and he has made him the head of the Church, which is his body, and which is the fullness of him who fills all in all. ∽

Ask for God's grace

Ask Mary here present to pray with you and for you for the grace she so much wants you to have: to know Jesus better not only as Lord, but as a loving Lord who loves you personally, so that you can love him more and follow him more closely. Ask the same grace from Jesus himself.

Prayer points

1. The Father has "chosen us in Christ before the foundation of the world to be holy and without fault before him in love." Before the world began, God chose you to exist as exactly the person you are now, choosing you out of all the possible persons you might have turned out to be. He chose you in Christ; with Jesus Christ in mind as well as you, the Father chose you out of love for you, and he chose you to live in love with and through Jesus Christ.

2. "He (the Father) has made him (Jesus) the head of the Church, which is his body, and which is the fullness of him…." The Church as the body of Jesus Christ holds the fullness of the presence and the power of the love of Jesus. The Church is the strongest zone of Jesus' presence and the power of his love.

3. The Church is "the fullness of him who fills all in all," the fullness of Jesus as Lord. The Lord Jesus fills all reality with his presence and with his love. Even though the strongest area of his presence is the Church itself, nevertheless the Lord Jesus is present filling with the power of his loving presence every part of the universe, "he fills all in all." He is a loving Lord, a Lord of love.

Closing prayer

Mary my mother, mother of my Lord, the Lord of all, help me to know Jesus better, to love him more, and to follow him more closely. Help me to always accept and profess Jesus as my personal Lord and Savior.

Lord Jesus, I adore you. I pray together with the Blessed Virgin Mary, your mother, whom you have given to me as my mother. You are Lord, the Lord God, the Lord of all things in heaven and on earth. I adore you and I thank you, because you are a loving Lord, who gave himself for me, out of love for me. Thank you, Jesus. Amen.

Short prayer to repeat during the day

Lord Jesus, you have chosen me.

Fifth Day
———

Jesus Is Lord of the Future

Thought of the future—that of the world and of my own personal future—can be full of hope and expectation or filled with fear. Our foundation, however, is that "We come through all these things triumphantly victorious, by the power of him who loved us. For I am certain that nothing already in existence, and nothing still to come...will be able to come between us and the love of God known to us in Christ Jesus" (Rom 8:37–39).

Acknowledge God's presence

In prayer acknowledge the presence of Jesus and Mary, both here now looking at you with love.

Read God's Word   EPHESIANS 1:11–12

In Christ we, who have been destined according to the purpose of him who works everything out according to his will and plan, have received our inheritance, so that we too, the first to set our hope on Christ, might live for the praise of his glory. 〜

Ask for God's grace

Ask Mary here present to pray with you and for you for the grace to know Jesus better as a loving Lord who holds your future in his hands and who loves you personally, so that you can love him more, follow him more closely, and put all your trust and hope in him. Ask the same grace from Jesus himself.

Prayer points

1. The Father's plans for the world and for me personally are built on and around Jesus Christ risen from the dead. Jesus is Lord of the future; both the future of the world and my future are in him. Jesus, now risen, transcends all time and space; he sees the future happening and he is its Lord. Paul calls Jesus "our hope" (1 Tim 1:1), and

says, "on him we have set our hope" (2 Cor 1:10). I hope in Jesus for the future.

2.	Jesus calls me to trust in him, to hope in him, to take seriously not only his love for me but also the power of that love. He is the Lord of my future. I can trust in him. I can hope in him for tomorrow, for next week, for the rest of my life, and for eternity.

3.	I do not know what the future holds, but I do know who holds the future. Jesus holds my future in his heart, hidden from me but known perfectly to him. He is the Lord of that future; nothing will happen that he does not will or permit to happen.

Closing prayer

Mary my mother, mother of my Lord, the Lord of all, help me to know Jesus better, to love him more, and to follow him more closely. Help me to trust him and hope in him in all matters.

Lord Jesus, I pray together with the Blessed Virgin Mary, your mother whom you have given to me as my mother. You are Lord, the Lord God, the Lord of the future. You are the Lord of my future. I adore you, I trust you, I hope in you, because you are a loving and powerful Lord. Amen.

Short prayer to repeat during the day

Lord Jesus, I trust you.

Putting Everything under the Lordship of Jesus

"**H**e (the Father) has put all things under his (Jesus') feet and has made him the head over all things" (Eph 1:22). "Then comes the end when he hands over the Kingdom to God the Father...for he must reign until he has put all his enemies under his feet" (1 Cor 15:24). "Jesus Christ—he who is the blessed and only Sovereign, the King of kings and Lord of lords" (1 Tim 6:15). This is the Lord who has chosen me in love.

Acknowledge God's presence

Both Jesus and Mary are here now looking at you with love. Acknowledge them in prayer.

Read God's Word   EPHESIANS 1:8–10

With infinite wisdom and understanding, the Father has revealed to us the mystery of his will according to the plan that he has put forth in Christ, a plan for the fullness of time. The plan is this: to recapitulate all things in Christ, everything in heaven, and everything on earth. ∼

Ask for God's grace

Ask Mary here present to pray with you and for you for the grace to know Jesus better as the loving Lord of your whole life and of every part of it, so that you can love him more, follow him more closely, and center your life on him. Ask the same grace from Jesus himself.

Prayer points

1. "The plan is this: to recapitulate all things in Christ." This is the plan not only for the world but also for me. Jesus wants me to center myself and everything in my life on him.

2. What worries me or concerns me at present? Jesus is interested in that. He cares about my worries and concerns. I put that under his lordship and give that problem to him.

3. Who rejects me or dislikes me or is angry at me or causes me problems? I can trustingly put that person and my relationship with that person under the lordship of Jesus, into his hands. It is his problem. Whom do I love selfishly, or possessively, or inadequately, or insufficiently? I put that person and my relationship with that person into Jesus' hands now, under his loving lordship, for him to heal and fill with his love, making the rough ways smooth and the crooked ways straight. What thoughts or feel-

ings distract and preoccupy me in prayer? If they distract me from him, they are not really under the lordship of Jesus; I can put them there now.

Closing prayer

Mary my mother and the mother of my Lord, the Lord of all, help me to know Jesus better, to love him more, and to follow him more closely. Help me to put everything under his lordship, into his hands.

Lord Jesus, together with the Blessed Virgin Mary, I come to you. You are Lord, the Lord God, the Lord of my life. I put myself, all my worries, concerns and problems, and all my relationships with other people under your lordship, into your hands. Amen.

Short prayer to repeat during the day

**All that I do, think, and feel now,
I put into your hands, Lord.**

Seventh Day

Jesus Is Lord in the Eucharist

The divine presence is everywhere, but uniquely in the Eucharist. Jesus is there body, blood, soul, and divinity. This is the holy presence that we celebrate, receive, and adore. The blinding glory of God is in the tabernacle, is on the altar. It is amazing that we are not struck down in this awesome presence. The radiance of God's glory blazes out from the altar—"glory like a consuming fire" (Ex 24:17). The Son, Jesus, whom we receive "is the radiance of God's glory" (Heb 1:3). Yet, Jesus calls us to come near: "It is I; do not be afraid" (Jn 6:20).

Acknowledge God's presence

Jesus and Mary are both here, loving you and helping you. Acknowledge them prayerfully.

Read God's Word   Matthew 26:26–28

While they were eating, Jesus took bread and gave thanks. He broke the bread, gave it to his disciples, and said: "Take this, all of you, and eat it. This is my body." Then he took the cup, gave thanks, and gave the cup to his disciples, and said, "Take this, all of you, and drink from it, this is the cup of my blood, the blood of the new covenant; it will be shed for many so that sins may be forgiven." ∽

Ask for God's grace

Ask Mary here present to pray with you and for you for the grace to know Jesus better so that you can love him more and follow him more closely, and center your life on him. Especially ask to know him in the Eucharistic celebration, and to know him in his Eucharistic presence as Lord. Ask the same grace from Jesus himself.

Prayer points

1. Jesus has risen, ascended into heaven, and is present to all of us now, always, everywhere. He is present in a special way, for your greater support, spiritual strength, and growth in the Sacrament of the Eucharist.

    In the Eucharistic celebration, Jesus is the one offered to the Father, together with the priest and the people. Jesus is the main offerer; he offers the celebration together with the priest and the people, all together with Jesus offering themselves and Jesus to the Father. Each person offers the celebration, too, although it is only the priest who says the words that Jesus said at the last supper.

    Every Eucharistic celebration is an offering, a sacrifice to the Father that draws its power from the sacrifice of the cross, where the Priest and the Offering were the same. But in the Eucharistic celebration, Jesus does not die; he is risen and he bears in his risen body the five wounds of his suffering and death on the cross. I can unite myself now with all the Eucharists being celebrated at this moment all over the world, offering myself as a gift with Jesus to the Father.

2. The Eucharist is a sacrifice. It repeats the last supper of Jesus and the disciples, which drew its power from the sacrifice of the cross that was to come.

Right now, I can offer up any suffering or problems I have, including them in the sacrifices of all the Eucharists being celebrated at this moment in the world. In that way I unite my sufferings and sacrifices to Jesus' sacrifice of the cross.

3. In sacramental Communion, Jesus comes to me in a special way, under the appearance of bread and wine. The Eucharistic celebration is an exchange of gifts. I have offered Jesus and myself with Jesus' offering to the Father; now the Father gives me the gift of Jesus in sacramental Communion.

Adoration of the Eucharist is an "extension" of sacramental Communion and so an "extension" of the Eucharistic celebration. Even if I am not now in a church, I can worship and adore Jesus present in the Eucharist, in his Eucharistic lordship, in churches all over the world right now.

Closing prayer

Mary my mother, mother of my Lord, the Lord of all, help me to know Jesus better, to love him more, and to follow him more closely. Help me to put everything under his lordship and into his hands.

Lord Jesus, together with the Blessed Virgin Mary, I come to you. You are Lord, the Lord God, the Lord of my life. I place myself and all my worries, concerns, and problems, all my relationships with other people under your lordship, into your hands. Amen.

Short prayer to repeat during the day

Jesus, Lord of my life.

Chapter V

Preparing
for
New Grace

During the next seven days, we want to receive new grace, new gifts, a new outpouring of the Holy Spirit. Sometimes, not wrongly but perhaps misleadingly, the new outpouring of the Holy Spirit for which we will pray is called the "baptism in the Holy Spirit." The so-called baptism in the Holy Spirit is not a sacrament, but something the Lord does in answer to prayer. The Lord answers our prayer by pouring out his Spirit into our hearts.

PRAYER FOR THE WEEK

First Day

Jesus Is Baptized in the Holy Spirit

Jesus went down to the Jordan where John was baptizing. John had prophesied: "I baptize you with water; but one who is more powerful than I is coming. He will baptize you with the Holy Spirit and with fire" (Lk 3:16). Jesus of course already had the Spirit in fullness, but from now on, the effects began to show: "Jesus full of the Holy Spirit returned from the Jordan and was led by the Spirit into the wilderness" (Lk 4:1). Later, Jesus, "filled with the power of the Holy Spirit, returned to Galilee" (Lk 4:14).

Acknowledge God's presence

Jesus and Mary are both here, loving you and helping you. Acknowledge them prayerfully.

Read God's Word   LUKE 3:21–22

　　After all the people had been baptized, and after Jesus too had been baptized and was praying, the sky opened. The Holy Spirit descended on Jesus in the material form of a dove. And a voice was heard speaking from the heavens, "You are my Son, and beloved; I am well pleased with you." $\sim$

Ask for God's grace

Ask Mary here present to pray with you and for you for the grace that you want: to know Jesus better so that you can love him more and follow him more closely, and the grace to be open to the Holy Spirit. Ask the same grace from Jesus himself.

Prayer points

1.　"The Holy Spirit descended on Jesus in the material form of a dove." Jesus here publicly and openly receives a new outpouring of the Holy Spirit. But did not Jesus have the Holy Spirit always? Yes, of course. Jesus was and is God, in union with the Father, in the unity of the Holy Spirit, one God. But in his human nature he grew in age, grace, and wisdom. Here Jesus receives, in his humanity, a new and transforming grace that he needs for his vocation, to answer the call of the Father, for his ministry.

2. A voice was heard speaking from the heavens, "You are my Son, and beloved; I am well pleased with you." Jesus is the image, the reflection, of the Father. He sees the Father always, and always does the Father's will.

3. The Holy Spirit descended on Jesus in the material form of a dove. Since the baptism of Jesus, the dove has become the traditional symbol of the Holy Spirit. The dove is free, it flies through the air where it wants, and it stands for peace. The Spirit of Jesus and the Father, the Holy Spirit, dwells in my heart now and gives me freedom from my worst tendencies, freedom to love, and peace in the depths of my heart. The Spirit relates me face to face with those whom he unites in himself: Jesus and the Father.

Closing prayer

Mary my mother, help me to know Jesus better, so that I can love him more and follow him more closely.

Lord Jesus, you were baptized in the Holy Spirit. Increase your Holy Spirit in my heart now, and pour out your Spirit on me so that I can be more closely united with you. Amen.

Short prayer to repeat during the day

Jesus, help me to know you better.

Jesus Sends the Holy Spirit at Pentecost

Once the apostles had received the Holy Spirit at Pentecost, they "set fire to the earth." Jesus said, "I have come to bring fire to the earth and how I wish it were already kindled" (Lk 12:49). These men who had run away when Jesus was arrested, who hid in the upper room with the door bolted after Jesus was killed, are now transformed into witnesses over all the earth, even to the laying down of their lives. "You will receive power when the Holy Spirit has come upon you, and you will be my witnesses to the ends of the earth" (Acts 1:8).

Acknowledge God's presence

Mary is here, loving you and helping you. Jesus is present with you, looking at you with love. Recognize their presence and begin your prayer.

Read God's Word   Acts 2:1–4

When the day of Pentecost had come, the disciples were together in the upper room. Suddenly from heaven came the sound of a violent wind; the sound filled the whole house in which they were. Tongues, like fire, appeared and then split and placed themselves over the heads of each one present. All of them were filled with the Holy Spirit and began to speak in tongues as the Spirit led them. ⌒

Ask for God's grace

Ask Mary here present to pray with you and for you for the grace to know Jesus better so that you can love him more and follow him more closely, and the grace to be open to the Holy Spirit. Ask for the same grace from Jesus himself.

Prayer points

1. "When the day of Pentecost had come…." The Holy Spirit descended not simply on a random day, but on a special religious feast day. God respects special times as times of grace. The day that you will pray for a new outpouring of the Holy Spirit is one such special time. Your worship in church is another. Your quiet time with the Lord every day is a special time of grace.

2. "Suddenly from heaven came the sound of a violent wind." Just as the Spirit appeared as a dove at the baptism of Jesus, so here Jesus himself sends his Spirit, and a violent wind is the symbol of the Spirit. The Holy Spirit is powerful, and like the wind he blows wherever he wants to. The Holy Spirit empowers me to relate to Jesus and to pray, to love, to avoid sin, and to serve the Lord.

3. "All of them were filled with the Holy Spirit." What does it mean to be filled with the Holy Spirit? It means to be

much more filled with the Holy Spirit than before. It means to receive new gifts, especially of witnessing by word and deed and by your life, witnessing to the Lord.

Before Pentecost, the disciples had seen the risen Jesus several times. They believed in him firmly and they loved him. But they had not yet received the Spirit, the "power from on high" that Jesus had promised would descend on them. So, they fearfully hid from the authorities, with good reason, in the upper room. Then the Holy Spirit empowered them, and they converted people, worked miracles, healed the sick, cast out evil spirits, spoke the Good News to others, and witnessed to the Lord by their lives. The power of the love of the Holy Spirit in their lives made a tremendous difference.

Closing prayer

Mary my mother, help me to know Jesus better, so that I can love him more and follow him more closely.

Lord Jesus, you sent the Holy Spirit at Pentecost. Increase your Holy Spirit in my heart now, and pour out your Spirit on me so that I can be more closely united with you, and be empowered by you through your Spirit to serve you and to witness to you in my life. Amen.

Short prayer to repeat during the day

Jesus, give me more of your Spirit of love.

Who Is the Holy Spirit?

We might call the Holy Spirit "the Knowledge of God," because "the Spirit searches the depth of God" (1 Cor 2:10–11). We received the Holy Spirit at our baptism. We grow more and more in the knowledge and love of God with every coming of the Holy Spirit. Every time we receive grace, the Holy Spirit comes. St. Thomas Aquinas says that a few times in our lives we can receive the Holy Spirit in a special way, as a great transforming grace that changes our lives. Jesus in his conversation with Nicodemus likened the Spirit to wind—one cannot see the wind, but one can feel it and see its effects. During this week, we are praying for a new outpouring of the Holy Spirit. The liturgy for the feast of the Holy Trinity says:

The Father is Love,
the Son is the Gift of Love,
the Holy Spirit is the Giving of the Gift
(second antiphon of the Office of Readings).

Acknowledge God's presence

Jesus and Mary are here, loving you. Acknowledge them.

Read God's Word   JOHN 14:15–17

Jesus said at the last supper, on the night before he died, "If you love me, you will keep my commandments. And I will ask the Father, who will send you another Advocate, to be with you for ever. This Advocate is the Spirit of truth. The world cannot receive him, because it does not understand him and it does not know him. You know him. He abides with you, and he will be in you." ∼

Ask for God's grace

Ask Jesus, through the intercession of Mary, for the grace to know Jesus better, to love him more, and to follow him more closely. Ask also for the grace to appreciate better the presence of the Holy Spirit who relates you to Jesus and unites you to him.

Prayer points

1. "I will ask the Father, who will send you another Advocate, to be with you forever." An advocate is one who supports, defends, protects, and guides—and especially one who pleads the cause of another. Sometimes lawyers are called advocates. Jesus is my Advocate, and he tells me that another Advocate, the Spirit, is already with me and is coming to me soon. "He abides with you, and he will be with you."

2. "The world cannot receive him, because it does not understand him and it does not know him." "The world" here is meant in a negative sense: the world of sin, the world that turned against the Lord and that rejected Jesus

when he came, that rejects or ignores him still. This is the world of sinfulness, of a "worldliness" that we want to avoid because it leads us away from the Lord. This is the world that tempts us. It is what is meant when we say that temptations come from the world, the flesh, and the devil. This is the world that we renounce so that we can know Jesus and have his Spirit live in us.

3. The Holy Spirit is the Spirit of truth, our Advocate, and he is especially the power of God's love. The angel says to Mary, "The Holy Spirit will come upon you, and the power of the Most High will overshadow you." This is a typical Hebrew parallelism: it means that the "Holy Spirit" *is* "the power of the Most High."

    Jesus moves in the power of the Holy Spirit. He tells the disciples to wait in the upper room until power from on high descends on them. The Holy Spirit empowers me, and will empower me even more to know Jesus better, to love him and others more, to follow Jesus more closely, and to serve him better in my brothers and sisters.

Closing prayer

Mary my mother, help me to know Jesus better, so that I can love him more and follow him more closely.

Lord Jesus, you sent the Holy Spirit at Pentecost. Increase your Holy Spirit in my heart now and pour out your Spirit on me so that I can be more closely united with you, and be empowered by you through your Spirit to serve you and to witness to you in my life. Amen.

Short prayer to repeat during the day

Jesus, you defend me and support me. Thank you.

What Does the Holy Spirit Do?

The Holy Spirit is God, the Third Person of the Blessed Trinity. In the Trinity, the Spirit is the mutual love between the Son and the Father. On the day of Pentecost Peter described the Holy Spirit as "gift." "Repent...be baptized...you will receive the gift of the Holy Spirit" (Acts 2:38). Since the Holy Spirit is the knowledge and the love of God that is what he effects in us. The Spirit gives us life (cf. 2 Cor 3:6). The Spirit intercedes for us before God, "When we do not know how to pray properly, the Spirit personally makes our petitions for us" (Rom 8:26). The Spirit is a "spirit of adoption, enabling us to cry out 'Abba, Father!'" (Rom 8:15). The Spirit brings us freedom: "Now this Lord is the Spirit, and where the Spirit of the Lord is, there is freedom" (2 Cor 3:17). Above all, God the Holy Spirit transforms us in prayer to the likeness of God, "All of us with our unveiled faces like mirrors reflecting the glory of the Lord are being transformed into the image that we reflect...this is the work of the Lord who is Spirit" (2 Cor 3:18).

Acknowledge God's presence

Through his Holy Spirit, Jesus is present to you and within you. Come into his presence. Ask Mary to help you to pray during this quiet time with the Lord.

Read God's Word   Romans 5:5

God's love has been poured into our hearts through the Holy Spirit who has been given to us. ∼

Ask for God's grace

Ask Jesus, through the intercession of Mary, for the grace to know him better, to love him more, and to follow him more closely. Ask also for the grace to appreciate better the presence of the Holy Spirit, who relates you to Jesus and unites you to him.

Prayer points

1. Who is the Holy Spirit? The Father loves Jesus; Jesus loves the Father. The love between them is infinitely strong, so strong it is a Divine Person, the Holy Spirit. He is Love, the mutual love between the Father and the Son. He is not only a relationship between two persons, he is also a person: God. The Father, the Son, and the Spirit are all God, in an infinitely close union of love.

2. The Holy Spirit dwells in my heart. As a result of the Spirit's dwelling in my heart, the change or changes in me are what we call grace: sanctifying grace that helps

me to be holy, actual grace that helps me in particular situations, and healing grace that heals me in various ways.

3. What does the Holy Spirit do? He acts in me and creates grace. Most importantly, the Spirit relates me directly to the Father and to Jesus, because he is the relationship of love between them.

Closing prayer

Mary my mother, help me to know Jesus better, so that I can love him more and follow him more closely.

Lord Jesus, you sent the Holy Spirit at Pentecost. Increase your Holy Spirit in my heart now, and pour out your Spirit on me so that I can be more closely united with you, and be empowered by you through your Spirit to serve you and to witness to you in my life. Amen.

Short prayer to repeat during the day

Lord Jesus, increase in me your Spirit of love.

Fifth Day

Mary and the Holy Spirit

"In Mary, the Holy Spirit *fulfills* the plan of the Father's loving goodness. With and through the Holy Spirit, the Virgin conceives and gives birth to the Son of God"

(*Catechism of the Catholic Church,* n. 723). Mary is the masterwork of the Son and Holy Spirit. "In her the 'wonders of God' that the Spirit was to fulfill in Christ and the Church began to be manifested" (*CCC,* n. 721). "She is the burning bush of the definitive theophany. Filled with the Holy Spirit she makes the Word visible in the humility of his flesh. It is to the poor and the first representatives of the gentiles that she makes him known.... Through Mary, the Holy Spirit begins to bring men, the objects of God's merciful love, *into communion* with Christ" (*CCC,* nn. 724, 725).

Acknowledge God's presence

Mary and Jesus are present. Thank them and begin your prayer.

Read God's Word   John 14:16

>   Jesus said, "I will ask the Father, and he will send you another Advocate." ⌁

Ask for God's grace

Ask Jesus, through the intercession of Mary, for the grace to know Jesus better, to love him more, and to follow him more closely. Ask also for the grace to appreciate better the presence of the Holy Spirit who relates you to Jesus and unites you to him, and to receive new graces, a new outpouring of the Holy Spirit.

Prayer points

1. We pray to Mary sometimes as "most gracious advocate." The Church, especially in the liturgy, sometimes applies words and phrases from the Bible to persons or situations other than those obviously intended by the Bible. In that tradition, we can apply these words of Jesus to his mother. He tells us that he sends her to us—to you and to me—as an advocate to defend, support, protect, and guide us and plead our cause.

2. Sometimes the word "advocate" in John's gospel is translated as "Paraclete." A paraclete is a comforter. The translation of the above text could then be: Jesus said, "I will ask the Father, and he will send you another Comforter or Paraclete." The Holy Spirit consoles and comforts us; so does Mary.

3. Mary brings the Holy Spirit and acts as a channel for the Holy Spirit. When she was pregnant with Jesus, she visited her cousin and brought the Spirit to Elizabeth and to the unborn John the Baptist. This is a paradigm of what she does for each of us.

Closing prayer

Mary my mother, help me to know Jesus better, so that I can love him more and follow him more closely.

Lord Jesus, you sent the Holy Spirit at Pentecost. Increase your Holy Spirit in my heart now, and pour out your Spirit on me so that I can be more closely united with you, and be empowered by you through your Spirit to serve you and to give better witness to you in my life. Amen.

Short prayer to repeat during the day

Mary, pray for me; lead me to Jesus.

The Conditions of Prayer

S t. Irenaeus says, "The Spirit prepares us for the Son of God; the Son brings us to the Father, and the Father bestows on us incorporation for eternal life which comes to us from our gazing on God," that is, from prayer.

Acknowledge God's presence

Praise the Lord for his new gifts, and come into his loving presence. Ask Mary to be there with her Son.

Read God's Word JUDE 1:20–21

But you, my dear friends, must build yourselves up on the foundation of your most holy faith, praying in the Holy Spirit; keep yourselves within the love of God and wait for the mercy of our Lord Jesus Christ to give you eternal life. ⤳

Ask for God's grace

Ask Mary, in her love of her Son, to obtain from Jesus graces of prayer for you. Ask Jesus for those graces, too.

Prayer points

1. Time is the first condition of prayer. The Lord is not a time-keeper. But we cannot develop a relationship with anyone, let alone come to love them, unless we meet often. Meet Jesus every day. The more two people love one another, the more they delight to spend time together. We need to be in the company of Jesus, and this is prayer. Jesus likes being with you: "The Lord delights in you" (Is 62:4).

2. Prayer is simply being with the Lord, so come to him. What happens then is up to him. Go the way the Lord leads you, and do not drown out the Lord with chatter. Give him a chance to speak, to love you, to console you, and even to reproach you. Above all, contemplate him in all his reality; be face to face with Jesus "looking on the invisible God" (Heb 11:27). If you pray in church, then have an active faith in the presence of the Eucharist, Jesus in his love reaching out to you. Just be there. Prayer is not something you do; it is what the Lord does if you are there.

3. Persevere in prayer on a daily basis. Do not give up because you feel nothing. You are there for Jesus' sake more than for any satisfaction of your own. Be there for him,

even if you feel neither his love nor any love of your own for him.

Jesus does love you, personally, calling you by name. When you pray you come into the gaze of his love, into his lovingly looking at you, delighting in you, whether you feel anything or not. "Keep yourself within the love of God" (Jude 1:20).

As for your love of him, yes, it may be that your love is weak, but being there for Jesus is already loving him; love is shown in deeds more than in words or expressed feelings. Being there *is* loving.

A regular place of prayer is a help to perseverance in prayer. St. John of the Cross advises us not to despise "the trysting place." Pray where, when, and how you pray best. But always be open to any changes the Lord may want.

Closing prayer

Thank you, Jesus, for baptizing me in your Holy Spirit. Teach me to pray, to be quietly with you, to put in time with you, to come into the gaze of your love for me and to persevere there. Amen.

Short prayer to repeat during the day

Thank you, Jesus, for loving me.

Abide in Me

J esus said: "ask and it will be given you" (Mt 7:7). We have asked for the Holy Spirit and for his gifts, especially gifts of prayer. We have the Lord's word: "If you then, bad as you might be, know how to give good things to your children, how much more will your heavenly Father give to you the Holy Spirit when you ask him" (Lk 11:13). If nothing seems to have happened yet, wait, for the Lord never refuses an answer. "That he will come is as certain as the dawn" (Hos 6:3).

Acknowledge God's presence

I never really have to "enter" the presence of God, as God is always present to me. But I can become more open to his presence: "You will fill me with joy in your presence" (Acts 2:28).

Read God's Word   JOHN 15:4

Abide in me, as I do in you. Just as a branch cannot bear fruit all by itself unless it remains part of the vine, so neither can you bear fruit unless you abide in me. ∼

Ask for God's grace

Ask Jesus for graces of prayer, and ask Mary your mother to take you with her to Jesus in constant prayer, teaching you how to pray.

Prayer points

1. You could pray about the biblical text concerning the vine: staying close to Jesus in prayer, united to him, drawing life from the vine, bearing fruit because of your union with him, and living your life in him.

2. Those who have been baptized in the Holy Spirit are almost without exception gifted with graces of contemplative prayer, that is, the simple regard, seeking his face, resting in his presence. The way into contemplative prayer varies. Some people come deeply into the prayer of contemplation through the rosary. If one took the beads out of their hands, they would be lost! The vocal prayer of the rosary brings them to contemplation of Christ in his life, death, resurrection, and glory.

3. We are branches of the vine, or, in another metaphor that Paul used, parts of Christ's body. In either case we live, grow, and work effectively only insofar as we live in Christ. The sacraments, especially the Eucharist, are the source of life for us. Daily prayer too is a spring of life. Without

it we wither, but with it we are available for the Lord to use us as he wishes.

Shortly after Jesus ascended into heaven, Peter and John were arrested, thrown in jail overnight, and then hauled before the "rulers, elders, and teachers of the law. Peter filled with the Holy Spirit spoke up…. When they (the assembled leaders) saw the courage of Peter and John, and realized they were unschooled, ordinary men, they were astonished and they took note that these men had been with Jesus" (Acts 4:8, 13). Their having "been with Jesus," explained everything to even the hostile authorities. To be with Jesus is for us, prayer.

Closing prayer

Mary, please guide me to turn to Jesus at every moment, in work, recreation, decision, need, grief, rejoicing. Help me to recognize Jesus as being truly alive to me.

Jesus, I thank you that you are always with me. Let me never lose the awareness of your presence. Amen.

Short prayer to repeat during the day

Thank you, Jesus, for being with me.

ABOUT THE AUTHORS

Robert Faricy, a Jesuit priest, is Emeritus Professor of Spirituality at the Pontifical Gregorian University, Rome. He has written over twenty books on Teilhard de Chardin, spirituality, healing, discernment, and Marian apparitions. He is an international retreat director and speaker.

Lucy Rooney, a Sister of Notre Dame de Namur in England, is author of a dozen books on prayer and on Marian apparitions. An international speaker and retreat director, Sr. Lucy contributes regular articles to Marian renewal magazines in England.

BOOKS & MEDIA

The Daughters of St. Paul operate book and media centers at the following addresses. Visit, call or write the one nearest you today, or find us on the World Wide Web, www.pauline.org

California
3908 Sepulveda Blvd, Culver City,
  CA 90230   310-397-8676
5945 Balboa Avenue, San Diego,
  CA 92111   858-565-9181
46 Geary Street, San Francisco,
  CA 94108   415-781-5180

Florida
145 S.W. 107th Avenue, Miami,
  FL 33174   305-559-6715

Hawaii
1143 Bishop Street, Honolulu, HI
  96813   808-521-2731
Neighbor Islands call: 800-259-8463

Illinois
172 North Michigan Avenue, Chicago,
  IL 60601   312-346-4228

Louisiana
4403 Veterans Memorial Blvd,
  Metairie, LA 70006   504-887-7631

Massachusetts
Rte. 1, 885 Providence Hwy,
  Dedham, MA 02026
  781-326-5385

Missouri
9804 Watson Road, St. Louis,
  MO 63126   314-965-3512

New Jersey
561 U.S. Route 1, Wick Plaza,
  Edison, NJ 08817
  732-572-1200

New York
150 East 52nd Street,
New York, NY 10022
  212-754-1110
78 Fort Place, Staten Island, NY
  10301   718-447-5071

Ohio
2105 Ontario Street, Cleveland,
  OH 44115   216-621-9427

Pennsylvania
9171-A Roosevelt Blvd,
  Philadelphia, PA 19114
  215-676-9494

South Carolina
243 King Street, Charleston, SC
  29401   843-577-0175

Tennessee
4811 Poplar Avenue, Memphis,
  TN 38117   901-761-2987

Texas
114 Main Plaza, San Antonio, TX
  78205   210-224-8101

Virginia
1025 King Street, Alexandria, VA
  22314   703-549-3806

Canada
3022 Dufferin Street, Toronto,
  Ontario, Canada M6B 3T5
  416-781-9131
1155 Yonge Street, Toronto, Ontario,
  Canada M4T 1W2   416-934-3440

¡También somos su fuente para libros, videos y música en español!